Teaching Drama in the Classroom

A Toolbox for Teachers

Edited by

Joanne Kilgour Dowdy
Kent State University, Ohio, USA

and

Sarah Kaplan
Kent State University, Ohio, USA

SENSE PUBLISHERS
ROTTERDAM / BOSTON / TAIPEI

A C.I.P. record for this book is available from the Library of Congress.

ISBN 978-94-6091-535-2 (paperback)
ISBN 978-94-6091-536-9 (hardback)
ISBN 978-94-6091-537-6 (e-book)

Published by: Sense Publishers,
P.O. Box 21858, 3001 AW Rotterdam, The Netherlands
www.sensepublishers.com

Some selections were printed with permission from the following journal publications:

Dowdy, J. (1999). Becoming the poem: How poetry can facilitate working across differences in a classroom. *The Change Agent. Adult Education for Social Justice: News, Issues and Ideas.* New England, MA: Literacy Resource Center.

Dowdy, J. (2002). Poetry in the middle school classroom: An artist/activist and teacher collaboration leading to reform. *Teacher Development*, 6(1), 105-128.

Dowdy, J. (2008). Radio story: Drama in the critical literacy classroom. *Excelsior: Leadership in Teaching and Learning*, 3(1), 111-121.

Dowdy, J. (2009). From poems to video script. *Excelsior: Leadership in Teaching and Learning*, 3(2), 56-71.

Dowdy, J. (2010). Poetry is motion. *Innovative learning strategies twentieth biennial yearbook 2009-2010* (pp. 13-28). Romeoville, IL: College Literacy and Learning Special Interest Group, IRA.

Printed on acid-free paper

TABLE OF CONTENTS

Adapting Literature

Storytelling

Creative Play

ANTHONY MANNA

INTRODUCTION

Teachers talk about drama:

> I think it's about critical thinking, like weighing options, considering the reper-
> cussions of your choices , exploring values … that sort of thing.
>
> Jennifer, high school English

> It's about social skills. Students learn the importance of listening and cooperat-
> ing and sharing ideas.
>
> LaToya, second grade

> I'm thinking social studies. In the skits and short plays, my kids are seeing
> history from the inside out. They're living it by stepping into others' lives and
> learning what happened from there.
>
> Mark, middle school

> I'm amazed how drama helps with reading, especially with comprehension and
> making inferences, you know, discovering ideas between the lines.
>
> Donnamarie, literacy coach

> Three boys in my class who have done almost nothing all year participated in
> the statue exercise. Even if this doesn't raise test scores, that's enough for me.
>
> Lynn, middle school

Witnessing firsthand the ways drama activity puts their students' imaginations
to work, these teachers experienced drama's value as a powerful teaching and
learning strategy that invites students of all ages to move collaboratively inside
classroom content, human issues, and significant events. When teachers harness
drama's power with accurate learning outcomes, a precise structure, and appropriate drama techniques, drama activity can become a fertile method for integrating
reading, writing, speaking, listening, researching, technology applications, and art
experiences. Inside the imagined space that is drama's domain, students use their
own lives and perceptions as a supply of ideas for taking on roles and through
their interactions with others, dramatizing and reflecting on the experiences and
circumstances which people face throughout a lifetime. Drama inspires students
to grapple with different – often opposing – points of view, beliefs and values,
to play out alternate solutions to human problems and dilemmas, and to understand the fundamental issues that enliven content area topics and themes – for the
purpose of gaining knowledge and the pleasure of developing awareness.

In a time of increased curriculum mandates and test pressures, to suggest to teachers that they draw on drama's dynamics to teach content and examine human issues may seem an untimely idea completely out of synch with school reality. With high-stakes testing and test-based accountability stark realities in their daily professional lives, it's only natural for teachers to ask, what's the point? Why should we take precious time in an increasingly jam-packed classroom agenda to add yet another subject like drama to our program? After all, isn't drama a better fit for teachers who have the talent for directing plays or coaching the drama club or directing the annual full-scale play production that attracts those eccentric and creative kids? Well, *educational* drama is less a subject or special interest than it is an art that can serve as a viable learning medium. And like any thoughtfully planned classroom strategy, drama has the potential to maximize rather than limit instruction while it also supports students' emerging discoveries about content and concepts, the human condition, and themselves as creative makers of ideas in interaction with others.

In *The Death and Life of the Great American School System* (2010), Diane Ravitch, premier education historian and former U.S. assistant secretary of education, passionately advocates for school reform that provides a secure place for the arts, including drama, in every grade. Ravitch is convinced that standardized testing, punitive accountability, and other contentious petitions for restructuring today's schools have become a mandate that narrowly defines what is essential for American students to learn throughout their time at school. What's often omitted these days, Ravitch posits, are sufficient experiences in aesthetic education. Referencing Richard Rothstein et al.'s *Grading Education*, she puts her critique in these skeptical terms: "By holding teachers accountable only for test scores in reading and mathematics ... schools pay less attention to students' health, physical education, civic knowledge, the arts, and enrichment activities" (p. 161). In the curriculum Ravitch envisions, "... all children deserve the opportunity to play a musical instrument, to sing, engage in dramatic events, dance, paint, sculpt, and study the great works of artistic endeavor from other times and places (P. 235). So, what are the benefits of this entitlement? "Through the arts," Ravitch claims, "children learn discipline, focus, passion, and the sheer joy of creativity" (p. 235).

Ravitch is not alone in her prescriptions for strengthening America's schools with a national curriculum that integrates literature, the sciences, civics, geography, history, foreign languages, and the arts. Ken Robinson, a pathbreaking educator and internationally acclaimed leader in the development of human potential, has for years been lobbying for a national education system that thrives on an expanded perception of human intelligence and academic achievement. While Robinson reveres the serviceable abilities and subjects promoted through conventional academic programs, he believes that an education system would far better prepare students to cope with this century's rapidly changing innovations in science, technology, and global thought if educators raised students' instruction in creativity, the arts, and the humanities to a status on par with the training currently provided in mathematics and the sciences, which dominates school life. Robinson's ongoing – and sobering – research among pundits in private industry has revealed that the skills and talents demanded of twenty-first century thinkers and doers are rooted in creative brainpower: "... people who can think intuitively, who are imaginative and innovative, who can communicate well, work in teams and are flexible, adaptable and self-confident" (Robinson, 2001, p. 52). Robinson urges teachers to nurture creative intelligence by welcoming their students into virtual and actual environments that provide them consistent and coherent opportunities to experiment, to play with ideas, to deal with alternate points of view, and to discover connections across pieces of information that at first may appear unrelated. "Creativity is a basic human attribute that must be nurtured among all people, not just among artists and scientists," Robinson insists. "The freedom to learn, to create, to take risks, to fail or ask questions, to strive, to grow ... is the ethic upon which the US was founded. Promoting creativity among all people of all occupations, economic classes and ethnic backgrounds is essential to the common good" (p. 195).

If there currently exists a teaching aid that breaks free from narrow and limited notions of what is basic and vital to facilitating learning in a spirit of innovation, imagination, inquiry, and risk, it is the book you are holding, *Teaching Drama in the Classroom: A Toolbox for Teachers*, edited by Joanne Kilgour Dowdy and Sarah Kaplan. This sensible resource describes more than 35 scenarios of teachers and students in early elementary grades through graduate school working together to craft drama events that draw out participants' creative energies, interpretations of curricular topics, and investigations of social, political, and personal concerns. Within these dramatic incidents teachers help their students to visualize their understanding through writing, reading, engaging in research, weighing options, considering alternatives, inferring consequences, and devising solutions to human problems and conflicts.

In all of these lesson plans, students ramp up their imaginations in order to move into their respective roles and collectively explore whatever topics, concepts, themes, or tensions surface as they navigate their way through the conditions and experiences that unfold in a scene, skit, improvisation, or in interrelated episodes. Yet, for all the information these teachers offer in the way of drama techniques – role playing, scripting, dialogue, audience participation, dramatic tension, improvisation, the strategic use of interaction, space, movement, and gesture, and the like – it may surprise some readers to discover that woven throughout this manual is a perception of drama that has little to do with fine tuning students' acting skills or turning out refined dramatic events. For these teachers, drama clearly is not about theatrics or stunning performance; it's about enriching a learner's life by making content accessible and memorable through an active, hands-on, collaborative exploration of ideas. Nor is the practice of using drama as a teaching method reserved only for teachers with special training or a flair for the dramatic. The teacher who is an effective drama leader makes use of the same skills she or he uses each day to organize, structure, and orchestrate classroom content and to rally students around the tasks at hand with an array of appropriate and meaningful teaching strategies.

Throughout this manual, teachers support learning with an impressive assortment of drama styles and techniques. The more than fifty methods that fill the manual's eight topical sections represent two prevailing strategies that govern the practice of educational drama. Both strategies speak to the needs and experiences of educators new to the practice as well as to those well versed in drama's advantages as a useful tool for fostering active learning through shared imagination, constructive interaction, and critical thinking.

The first type of drama process pursued in this manual culminates with some sort of informal presentation. While a polished performance is rarely the intended goal of educational drama, make no mistake about the appeal and usefulness of low-key performance with even the most spontaneous or briefest classroom drama experience. In many of the manual's plans, for example, students work in small groups to prepare and rehearse their interpretation of a human condition, literary character, historical phenomenon, or subject area concept, which they then exhibit for their peers' edification, enjoyment, and response. A student-generated or commercial script frequently guides the presentation with a fixed structure, stage directions, dialogue, speaker direction, and other elements that distinguish play scripts from other types of written works. When this process occupies students, the enticement of working up an interesting and, as often happens, intriguing presentation serves as an incentive for them to be earnest about their commitment to the assignment, which, in turn, motivates them to closely examine different features of the topic from different angles.

As the manual's writers suggest, when the material interests students, the stakes are high, the outcomes clear, and the spirit of cooperation secure, students involved in a scripted and performance experience are positioned to learn a great deal from the drama process. Such is the case in Karen Elaine Seipert's chapter, "Developing Literature through Drama." Seipert initiates the process to help her high school students understand the characteristics of literary texts, particularly the characteristics of play scripts. They do this by transforming narrative selections into detailed radio scripts, represented in the chapter by complete scripts for their clever adaptations of Poe's "The Fall of the House of Usher" and Shakespeare's *The Taming of the Shrew*.

A scripting process moves students into a vast range of topics in "Radio Story Drama," Joanne Kilgour Dowdy's chapter. Dowdy directs her students to analyze incidents in newspaper articles as a catalyst for developing and rehearsing short scripts which they then present in audio recordings. In the samples Dowdy provides, students reworked an article about a sports rivalry, a political feature dealing with nuclear arms, and a clash between art collectors into spare satiric and ironic scenarios. Given the topical diversity found in journalism, Dowdy's approach holds much promise for dramatizing content across an entire curriculum.

For Mary Weems in "Don't Forget to FLY: Using Drama to Inspire Self-Esteem," script-making empowers high school females to discover and celebrate their special attributes. Weems integrates visualizing and imaging with writing in response to prompts, discussion about characteristics of dramatic writing and performing, and the use of thematic props as scaffolds to support her students as they prepare brief scenes that express sensitive personal revelations in a safe and protective workshop setting. Compassionate concern trumps indifference here through Weems's management of student engagement with self-illuminating behaviors.

In "Scripting Success: Using Dialogue Writing to Help Doctoral Students to Find Their Voice," the erratic emotional and intellectual life of graduate students is examined through Susan V. Iverson and Rhonda S. Filipan's tactics for using self-reflective writing, scripting, and performing to forge new understandings and adopt new awareness. Based on studies that clarify the importance of reflective writing for allowing students to makes sense of their academic experience, the authors propose that "Writing scripts and dialogues may allow doctoral students to give voice to powerful emotions, especially in a research-intensive environment that rewards objectivity rather than self examination." Iverson and Filipan then set into motion their poignant writing-performing process with inventive prompts that, for example, engage an individual's heart and head in dialogue about salient challenges of graduate school life or that asks the academic self to speak with a different facet of one's self or personality.

The second type of educational drama posited in this manual is largely open-ended. Under its influence, students engage in one-of-a-kind impromptu enactments or extensive improvisations laid out in structured, yet flexible inter-related episodes or scenes. Given that both of these approaches are essentially unscripted, students need to invent dialogue, actions, and interaction when they enter an episode and dramatize the lives of imagined characters in order to analyze and reflect on events from the characters' perspectives.

Although the teaching plan for each approach – short impromptus or multilayered improvisations – typically suggests a rudimentary course of action, a setting, recommended roles, and a basic storyline, the participants' ideas and discoveries about the topic being investigated within the drama often become the incentives for having the drama take unexpected turns. In fact, teachers who favor improvisation encourage participants to help shape the drama by freely interpreting a role and proposing new roles, or by suggesting the introduction of an unplanned event or episode – all for the sake of maintaining interest, strengthening student commitment, and deepening student understanding of the social condition, human event, or subject matter being examined. Taking note of these suggestions, teachers may decide to deviate from their original plans and move an improvisation they are facilitating or that students are processing independently in an unanticipated direction with different characters, a newly discovered conflict, or a different "real world" context that is a parallel reality to the drama's context.

Granted, its unpredictability may seem to make improvisation a risky classroom enterprise. Yet, as the teachers in this text make clear – the majority of whom endorse improvisational drama – the excitement, ownership, empowerment, cooperation, and, yes, *learning* – students experience with open-ended forms of drama, far outweigh the concern that the uncertainty upon which improvisation thrives will inhibit productive learning experiences. These teachers imply that every student, particularly ones who struggle academically, can tap the creative energy and problem solving skills fostered by improvisation. With Ken Robinson, they believe that "Creativity is not a special quality confined to special people and it can be taught" (p. 114). That's because all students are capable of putting their imaginations to work in response to the exhilarating question that sets every improvisation – indeed, every dramatic event – into motion: "What would happen if ...? In this manual, for example, "What would happen if ... a group of concerned black and white citizens protest racial segregation in 1960 in the south and clash with other citizens who detest segregation?," ask Janet Hill and Anthony L. Manna in their chapter, "Exploring History's Human Dilemma with Process Drama: Ruby Bridges and the Struggle for School Desegregation." In their multifaceted improvisational drama, the authors incorporate the roles of imagined and actual folks of the time and electronic slides of events and settings of the struggle in order to recreate the moral and political themes of a volatile and courageous transformation in America's social and political history.

In "Government Story Board," John Yurkschatt tempts readers to wonder, "What would happen if ... middle school students are invited to interpret the three branches of the US federal government with skits, songs, tableaux (still pictures), and storytelling?" After doing research on their respective branches, his students, working in small groups, devise story boards that they then present to their peers in inventive improvisations.

The premise of Mary Toepfer's chapter, "Bring the Story to Life: Using Drama with Literature," is "What would happen if teachers use improvisation as a pre-reading strategy with students who are preparing to enter some pretty dense texts by, say, Frederick Douglass and William Shakespeare?" In the open-ended episodes Toepfer designed, her students assume roles that, for example, stir them to examine slavery from many deeply moving perspectives. In her carefully structured pre-reading approach to *Macbeth*, students engage in a complex improvisation in which actual lines from the play's dialogue are incorporated in a contemporary situation and conflict that parallel the play's.

"What would happen if ... deaf students paired up with hearing peers to explore their respective cultures?" Carol L. Robinson and her co-authors ask in their chapter, "A Lesson for Merging Cultures." In pairs, then, their students move through incrementally arranged activities that include pantomime warm-ups, place-to-place movement, role play, and vivid sustained gesture to face the ambiguities, uncertainties, and illuminations that people can meet head-on when they cross cultural boundaries. Seize the opportunity here for using improvisation to make students culturally aware by positioning them inside the experiences of both young and older folks from various cultures not their own!

And so it goes in this wise book! Whether these teachers are endorsing scripted presentations or unscripted improvisations, they serve up a durable assortment of teaching plans that promise to entice students to take full advantage of their creative abilities and move into and reflect on content, concepts, relationships, and incidents. That their inspiring drama strategies come directly from actual experiences with students – in the early grades and up into graduate school – helps explain the feeling of authenticity that is woven like a sturdy thread through the fabric of each chapter. "You try it, too," the authors seem to be saying. Try it for the joy of the intense student involvement, communication, and self-confidence drama delivers. But try it, as well, for the cognitive and social skills and the perceptions and empathy it inspires.

In pressing their rationale for drama's goals as a compelling teaching and learning medium, the manual's authors affirm what many researchers have discovered about the range of skills supported by educational drama through observations of drama practice in classrooms and other venues (Wagner, 1998; Brown and Pleydell, 1999; Grady, 2000; Anderson, Cameron, and Carroll, 2009). Much like claims made in this book, research evidence asserts that, among other abilities, participation in drama activity encourages students and teachers to:

- integrate concepts, skills, and ideas from various subject areas, including social students, mathematics, science, and literacy;
- gain an understanding of real world events from the past and the present, the individuals who shaped these events, and the individuals who may influence them in the future;
- develop reading comprehension skills by entering the world of a text through role playing, interacting with others, visualizing events, concepts, and information, and dramatizing the experiences of fictional characters and real-life individuals;
- produce written works in a variety of contexts for different audiences that demonstrate increasing technical skill, self-confidence, and effective management of multimodal and electronic texts;
- discover and scrutinize ethical aspects of social issues such as equity, social justice, citizenship, civil rights, bigotry, bullying, and other forms of antisocial behavior and their reversals from various points of view;
- generate and use spoken, written, visual, and multimodal texts that demonstrate increasing fluency in the way of vivid description, sensory details, and effective persuasive and self-reflective writing;
- understand and develop compassion for others' representations of ideas, values, beliefs, experiences, and life conditions –from literary characters and challenged individuals to historical figures);
- acquire critical thinking skills in terms of examining, questioning, and perhaps challenging social practices and the language, actions, and beliefs that drive these practices, and investigating and evaluating texts concerning their manner of representing certain people, groups, and notions of reality;
- gain social skills through group problem solving, listening to differing views, respecting, weighing, and perhaps acting on another's proposals, and expressing empathy and compassion; and
- develop appreciation for the art of drama and theater.

In an era when educators are too often obliged to sacrifice the aesthetic and moral aims of education to only those manifestations of learning and teaching that can be quantified, scored, and tabulated, it's invigorating to come across a text that offers educators sound advice from the practice of professionals like themselves. They are, after all, a group of professionals that has discovered valid and reliable strategies for unlocking the inherent creativity of students and channeling that power into a dynamic process that has all the potential to make learning enjoyable and memorable. Welcome to *Teaching Drama in the Classroom: A Toolbox for Teachers*!

REFERENCES

Anderson, M., Cameron, D., & Carroll, J. (2009). *Drama education with digital technology*. New York: Continuum.

Brown, V. & Pleydell, S. (1999). *The dramatic difference: Drama in the preschool and kindergarten classroom*. Portsmouth, NH: Heinemann.

Grady, S. (2000). *Drama and diversity: A pluralistic perspective for educational drama*. Portsmouth, NH: Heinemann.

Ravitch, D. (2010). *The death and life of the great American school system: How testing and choice are undermining education*. New York: Basic Books.

Robinson, K. (2001). *Out of our minds: Learning to be creative*. Chichester, West Sussex: Capstone.

Wagner, B. J. (1998). *Educational drama and language arts: What research shows*. Portsmouth, NH: Heinemann.

CHARACTER DEVELOPMENT

YUKO KURAHASHI

AUTOBIOGRAPHICAL REPORT: PRESENTING YOUR RESEARCH USING THE FIRST-PERSON NARRATIVE

RATIONALE: RESEARCH AND PRESENTATION WITH A SENSE OF RESPONSIBILITY AND COMMITMENT

I invented this exercise using an autobiographical story-telling technique which I learned from "D'Lo," a Los Angeles based Tamil Sri Lankan-American, political theatre artist/writer, who came to our department as a guest lecturer. The first exercise in her workshop was to partner with another participant and to listen to each other's story. Then each participant told his/her partner's story in the first person. I was intrigued by this exercise, because I found a real sense of connection between myself and my exercise partner, who told her story in the first person using "I." The workshop participants also developed a sense of responsibility to tell accurately the other person's story, because they were telling it as that very person. This sense of responsibility led the participants to become more attentive to the information given by their partners and to try to present convincingly as the subject.

Autobiographical writing and presentation have become popular in academia in the past two decades as a vehicle to explore one's identity and subjectivity. In this first-person narrative exercise, we move beyond our own identity and sub-jectivity, by learning about the other participants and their experiences and then stepping out of our own identity to take the role of the other participant in telling their story. My version of this exercise is a means to develop the same sort of responsibility toward the subject of their research, that is, to know the subject and to tell its story as accurately and clearly as the participant/researcher can augment the depth and quality of research and writing.

WHAT TO DO

1. Ask students to choose a research topic.
2. Do research using the internet and at least one book/article found in the library.
3. Write a short introductory essay that explains the topic/subject, using the first-person narrative.
4. Present the essay in front of the class.

J.K. Dowdy and S. Kaplan, Teaching Drama in the Classroom, 11–12.

SAMPLE: WINNIE THE POOH

My name is Winnie the Pooh. I was born in 1926 on Cotchford Farm at the home of A.A. Milne. Telling my stories helped him to become famous as a "master" of children's literature; prior to 1926 he had been primarily known as a playwright. Pooh in Milne's stories was not as nice as the later version popularized in the Disney film. I am actually very greedy and surrounded by weird friends like Eeyore the Donkey, who is misanthropic, timid Piglet, and Owl, who has to do everything by the book. I became a "visible character" through the work of Ernest H. Shepherd, the original illustrator for the Pooh stories. Mr. Shepherd was an amazing man who traveled around the world on the income he earned illustrating for children's books. The licensing rights to The Winnie the Pooh stories were bought by Stephen Slesinger, an American radio, film and television producer. In 1961 Disney acquired the right from Slesinger to produce a film based on the Pooh stories and to create articles of merchandise based on the characters. I, along with my friends, became a famous Disney character. I appeared in several films, including *Winnie the Pooh and the Honey Tree, Winnie the Pooh and the Blustery Day* and *Winnie the Pooh and Tigger Too.*[1] However, in 1991 the Slesinger estate sued Disney for rights infringement, and I was at the center of the lawsuit, until September 2009 when the Federal District Court in Los Angeles dismissed the lawsuit.[2] In addition to this lawsuit, Mr. Milne's granddaughter tried to terminate the license granted to Stephen Slesinger in 2006. She is the daughter of Christopher Robin Milne after whom the character of "Christopher Robin" was named. The reason for her lawsuit was that she felt that both the Slesinger estate and the Disney Company ignore the important values in the original stories in their search for profit.[3]

I don't want to share only bad news about me, however. In recent years I have been very active in education, becoming a very effective pedagogical subject. For example, Charles A. Walker says that reading Winnie the Pooh is a great way to teach children two main epistemological positions – empiricism and rationalism.[4] I am very happy to know that I have been useful not only as an entertainer in children's books and the Disney movie, or as a "subject" of lawsuits. I believe in the importance of exploring a plurality of thoughts, ideas and backgrounds, and it is good to know some educators are using me and my friends to promote it.

---

[1] "Winnie the Pooh," *From Abba to Zoom: A Pop Culture Encyclopedia of the Late 20th Century,* Riverside, NJ: Andrews McMeel Publishing (2006), p. 532.

[2] Dave Itzkoff, "'Winnie-the-Pooh' Suit Is Dismissed," *New York Times* 30 September 2009. Late Edition. 2.

[3] "Attempt by Granddaughter of Author of 'Winnie-the-Pooh' Books to Terminate Grant to Licensee Stephen Slesinger, Inc., Was Not Effective, Court of Appeals Affirms," *Entertainment Law Reporter* 27.11 (April 2006), p. 6.

[4] Charles A. Walker, "Winnie-the-Pooh and Epistemology, too," *The Journal of Theory Construction & Testing* 11.1 (2007), p. 5.

JOANNE KILGOUR DOWDY

PICTURE THIS: DRAMA AND POETRY FOR PLAY

RATIONALE

The purpose of this workshop is to give students an interactive experience with drama in the classroom. They read, perform and dramatize the themes in selected poems to enhance the kinesthetic approach to learning. Based on the belief that human beings are all players who "act out" and that such a means of communication is natural and important to our successful functioning, the poetry performance workshop also encourages teachers to bring their own experiences to the classroom and develop ways to connect with their students through enacting stories.

WHAT TO DO

1. The teacher shares six selected poems with the participants.
2. The teacher instructs the students to choose the poem that inspires them.

   a) Participants choose one of the poems presented, forming six separate groups.
   b) In groups, the participants decide how best to represent the theme of the poem in tableaux. Each student must choose a character to represent.
   c) Groups look at each other's pictures.
   d) Answering the questions who, what, when, where and why will help each person talk about the character that he or she represents in the picture. Each group creates a character sketch for each of the people who appeared in the picture. The sketch may be a tracing of a face that they find in a magazine, newspaper article, or poster for an advertisement. The sketch is for an individual's poem. The use of the steps that describe the *Cycle of the Character's Story* are necessary in this part of the exercise.
   e) Participants then decide who gets which words from the poem to perform during the showing of the tableaux. The group rehearses the oral presentation.
   f) The group performs the poem in character for the class.
   g) Participants are invited to put their poems to music and perform the "lyrics" in character as they stand in the picture that represents the poem.

J.K. Dowdy and S. Kaplan, Teaching Drama in the Classroom, 13–14.

Cycle of the Character's Story

In order to create a character's history, the class is invited to go through a series of creative writing exercises. These include the following directions:

1. Choose a character from the image that you are using as a prompt.
2. Decide on a crisis event or wounding, learning or discovery that your character experiences in the course of his or her life. For example, if your character has had a parent die, it would be considered a wounding event. Try to fill in as many details as possible about the critical event that the character has endured.
3. Finally, create a scenario in your mind's eye about the way in which the critical incident is now applied to the character's life, that is, how does he or she use the learning or discovery to resolve new crises? Write as much as you can about this learning and its application to the character's life (Personal conversation with Jacqueline Peck, March 21, 2008).

These steps were designed to help the students think independently and to give the teachers some choices in their development of the theme. Participants may use them to connect with the artist's intentions and make choices, for example, play a statue, imagine the life of a statue, and then write about what it was like talking as the character of the statue.

RESULTS

The students had to ask questions of the poet, the poem, themselves and their classmates in order to construct realistic personae for their final project (Thomson, 2003). Individual learners showed their attitudes to life experiences, which allowed teachers to learn more about them and, therefore, respond to their needs on a more personal basis (Noddings, 1994). A family atmosphere developed in the classrooms as a result of the kind of listening and performances that students created around their characters. Quiet students found a way to share their inner lives, and outgoing students developed a way to use words to help paint their complex realities. A climate based on mutual respect for each other's work as collaborators became evident.

SARAH KAPLAN

STARTING FROM SCRATCH: CREATING DYNAMIC CHARACTERS

INTRODUCTION

I have found that students are much more engaged in learning if they have a personal connection to the subject matter. When I ask my students to create characters, they often don't know where to begin, so I started using a method of character creation that allows them to begin with information that they know: characteristics of themselves. While I use this lesson in my Acting classes, it could certainly be used in any language arts class as an introductory activity to character development. The goal is that each student will generate a list of nouns that relate to his life and adjectives that describe him. He will then give that list to another student who will create a first-person character monologue from the list of words. Students enjoy this activity, because they have a clear prompt to work from when they are doing the writing, and they end up with characters that are based on themselves. They love seeing the characters that their classmates invent from the details of their lives.

PROCEDURE

1. Ask each student to fold a piece of paper "hotdog style" (vertically). Students should not put their names on their papers, but they should put their gender.
2. Each student should write ten nouns that relate to him in column one. These can be descriptive nouns (friend, son, sister, scholar, actor, athlete or material items such as cell phone, running shoes, IPOD, peanut butter).
3. Each student should write ten adjectives that describe him in column two.
4. The teacher collects each paper and then re-distributes them so that each student has a new paper that IS NOT his or hers.
5. The students should create a monologue in first-person voice of a character based on the 20 words on the page. They should be true to the gender. They must give the character a name and, of course, an age. They do not need to use all (or any) word from the original writer. We are NOT looking for a re-listing of the words. What we want is a creative character based on the adjectives and nouns provided, but, of course, students can add their own details, as long as they make sense in comparison to the 20 words provided. The characters can be of any age, from any location, and with any job.

J.K. Dowdy and S. Kaplan, Teaching Drama in the Classroom, 15–16.

6. The teacher collects the monologues after they are finished. At this point, there are some options based on the personalities in the class:

   a) The teacher may read the monologues out loud and guess who the character is based on.

   b) The teacher may return the monologues to the original writer of the words (he or she has to read the words out loud in order to match them up) and allow students to read on their own.

   c) The teacher may return the monologues to the original writers of the words and have THEM read their monologues out loud.

7. The students discuss their feelings about the exercise. Did their characters sound anything like themselves? What makes these characters unique and interesting?

OPTIONAL FOLLOW-UP ACTIVITIES

1. In my acting class, I partner up the students, and they have to create a dialogue for their two characters and then perform it.

2. The teacher may also have students in groups create a story that involves all their characters.

3. Since the monologues end up being short and concise, there is always room to add more details. Each student may re-craft the monologue into a longer written piece with more information about the character.

JOANNE KILGOUR DOWDY

CARNIVAL CHARACTERS IN THE CLASSROOM

RATIONALE

This is a kinesthetic approach to teaching about carnival characters from Trinidad and Tobago like Midnight Robber, Dame Lorraine, and Jab Jab, in order to help students appreciate these archetypes. Using the reading theory of Vacca and Vacca (2002) sets up an environment where participants reflect on background knowledge about a subject, generate questions that they want to learn, and then consider the actual knowledge that has been gained after an experience with new material, are included. The workshop helps to uncover underlying personality characteristics that are represented in these carnival characters.

WHAT TO DO

Steps of the workshop: define the characters, have them improvise speeches with each other, have them mirrored in movement by the volunteers, decide on the stories that individual scenes should tell, have the stories told in movement, let the characters find their dance. Reflect on the stories and how they were resolved.

The following presents the five blocks that was developed, in my role as artist collaborator, at the planning meeting on our Carnival Character Development unit.

Step 1: Introduction to the Carnival Character Workshop

- Students would look at descriptions of the Jab Jab, Pierrot Grenade, Midnight Robber and Jamette; and look for clues to the character's "voice" in the text.
- The students would do small scenes where they experimented with the traditional movement style of each character.

The scenes are created when the group decides on a beginning, middle, and end of a short story that involves the characters. Each character has to determine what movement style represents their attitude, i.e. a "sexy" walk can be used for the Jamette, or a Midnight Robber might act like a bully, pointing his fingers in people's faces and shouting all the lines in his scene. All the students should have lines or reactions, in their body language, during the scene that is depicted.

J.K. Dowdy and S. Kaplan, Teaching Drama in the Classroom, 17–20.

Step 2: Practice with Carnival Characters

Activities would lead students to:

— Identify with the character's "voice." This can be facilitated if students first talk about a person or movie character who acts like a bully, harlot, evil and sinister antagonist, or verbose and nerdy person.

Then the students can be led in an improvised discussion where they have to say everything in a voice that reflects the character's attitude, i.e. shouting all the time for the Midnight Robber, or whispering in a sinister tone as Jab Jab.

Students can choose a situation where two characters meet and have to come to a decision about a problem that they want to solve. They could think about two people stuck in an elevator and they talk out their options in the voice of each character.

— Decide on the "point" of the carnival character, and the attitude of the person who would move like the character.

— Talk and write about the story that is being told through the carnival character.

Step 3: Choosing the Carnival Character

— Students will find out about the character; doing research on the history, geography, and events that are depicted in the carnival character.

— Students will find a person or community that they can compare to the person/events in the carnival character.

— Students will interview with someone in the community who reminds them of the character. Write about the way that you identify with the character/community; do improvised scenes in class in character; write "as if" you were the character (i.e., diary entries, newspaper editorials, letters to loved ones, etc.).

Step 4: Rehearsal of Characters

— Students will role play in couples to develop the "voice" of the character, i.e. the body language, the dialect, the clothing choices, etc.

— Teachers will put characters in situations and let them improvise their reaction by speaking with someone whom they just met (i.e., on the phone, at the mall, on the street looking for a house they have never seen before).

— Students will write about the experiences that came out of the improvisations based on character and situation.

18

Sample:

What We Know, Wanted to Know, and Learned

Following the KWL (Vacca et al., 2003) procedure for improved reading compre-hension i.e. Develop a chart that asks: What do you know? What do you want to know? What did you learn? We invited the audience to brainstorm some words and images that they associated with the carnival characters Pierrot Grenade, Jab Jab, Midnight Robber and Jamette. We then invited volunteers to come onto the stage and move around in the physical style of the carnival character that they wanted to depict. After looking at the volunteers move around in character, we froze the action on stage by asking the actors to hold their positions in some kind of statue that represented the personae of the four personalities that they represented.

The group then defined the characteristics of these personalities represented in the statutes that the actors depicted on stage, i.e. (a) Pierrot Grenade is similar to a mako or gossip; (b) Jab Jab acts like a devil or imp; (c) Jamette has the personality of a whore; and (d) Midnight Robber acts like a dangerous thief. Further, the group went on to identify the body language of these characters as depicted by the actors in their improvised scenes with each other. Because of our understanding of each carnival character's nature, i.e. they represented broad characterizations of the whore, the gossip, the thief, and the imp, we saw that the ways in which each person/character chose to communicate their ideas to other people, i.e. through language patterns and body movements, was dominated by the individual's intention or motivation. The physical language that the audience saw was a result of the internal monologue that the character was creating. The character's motivation, or psychology, expressed itself in the body language and speech that it chose to communicate with others, i.e. lascivious movement for the whore; intimidating gestures for the Midnight Robber.

What we wanted to know. What we wanted to know was defined in the question of what would happen when we put these characters in a setting with a teacher character. We knew that the characters would bring their personalities to the setting, using the body language and speech that represented their attitudes to life, and we also wanted to know what the teacher would provide under certain conditions with personalities who acted like whores, thieves, imps, or gossips.

Talking in character. Talking in character helped us realize the goal of the teacher workshop, i.e. to help teachers identify with the attitudes of their students who had characters similar to Jab Jab, Pierrot Grenade, Midnight Robber and Jamette. From the improvisations that the participants presented we could see that it was very hard for some teachers to maintain the attitude of the character if the teacher's personality was different from the attitude that the character represented. During the dramatic scenes that were improvised between the carnival characters that the teachers represented, the group and the actors realized that actors could not say things that were uninformed, or not determined by a logical approach to a character's attitude. For example, if the actor indicated that the carnival character

Jab Jab was an imp and inclined to be mischievous in the classroom, the actor could not act as if he was an easy going, passive human being in the improvisation he created with the teacher on stage.

Characters in improvisations. The "reality test" that the interview situations with characters provided brought home a clear idea – to the teachers and the workshop leaders. First, we noted that while the character's reality is based on imagination to some degree, i.e. what does a person who acts like an imp, an instigator of mischief, really want from other people in a relationship?, there must be a logic to the way that the imagined reality is organized in a dramatic scene. In other words, if you want your audience to believe your character's attitude, you are responsible for building that credibility on a firm foundation of body language and speech that convinces the onlookers of the inner monologue and a desire to have power in a given situation. An imp cannot behave like a whore in this dramatic exercise designed to get participants to identify with the characters.

What we learned. The teachers became actors in this journey, working through the upper levels of Bloom's taxonomy, particularly analysis and synthesis, as they brought characters to life in the workshop (Bloom, 1971). This integration of arts in learning furthered the underlying understanding that organized the drance (a combination of dance and drama methods) project in the carnival workshop. Those teachers who did not identify with their carnival character's autobiography, expressing a life through the body language and speech, had a difficult time committing their imaginations to the process of the dramatic improvisations. In contrast, those who invested their imaginations and critical thinking reached a very deep understanding of the concepts that the dance and drama symbols offered them to express their interpretation of human motivation and its effects on relationships in the classroom.

JOANNE KILGOUR DOWDY, MARTHA ABBOTT-SHIM, LYNN BRIGGS,
FLORENCE HARDNEY-HINDS & TRACY WOODHALL

PLAYING FOR CHARACTER DEVELOPMENT *

INTRODUCTION

The goal of the workshop was to help students build a repertoire of skills that facilitated their ability to identify the characters in poems and then perform the poems using the voice and physicality of the people they created. A series of classes were co-planned by the artist, who describes herself as a University Fellow at Middle School, and three other teachers at the school. The University Fellow implemented several of the features for successful involvement with the faculty and students, which are described in Delpit's "Ten Factors Essential to Success in Urban Classrooms" (L. Delpit, personal communication, 1998).

TEN FACTORS ESSENTIAL TO SUCCESS IN URBAN CLASSROOMS

1. Do not teach less content to poor, urban children, but understand their brilliance and teach more!
2. Whatever methodology or instructional programme is used, demand critical thinking.
3. Assure that all children gain access to "basic skills," the conventions and strategies that are essential to success in American education.
4. Provide the emotional ego strength to challenge racist societal views of the competence and worthiness of the children and their families.
5. Recognize and build on strengths.
6. Use familiar metaphors and experiences from the children's world to connect what they already know to school knowledge.
7. Create a sense of family and caring.
8. Monitor and assess needs and then address them with a wealth of diverse strategies.
9. Honor and respect the children's home culture(s).
10. Foster a sense of children's connection to community, to something greater than themselves.

---

* Parts of the article were first published under: Dowdy J. (2002). Poetry in the middle school classroom: An artist/activist and teacher collaboration leading to reform. *Teacher Development*, 6(1), 105–128.

This project developed into a 9-week unit of drama exercises and writing activities that supported the development of writing skills. The point of the exercise was to open a space in the classroom where students felt free to bring in their home language and celebrate it. This kinesthetic approach to teaching (Dowdy, 1999) became an opportunity to observe students who were successful at learning by doing. Among the items that we played with during the teacher-training session prior to working with their students, were my film frame/acting/writing exercise as described in the steps that follow.

POETRY SELECTIONS

I developed a series of lessons that helped students explore poetry from an actor's perspective. The steps led them to identify the character in a poem and then to demonstrate their understanding of the character through the performance of the poem.

With these ideas in mind, I provided choices of poetry from authors that included Langston Hughes, Marge Piercy, Beah Richards, Paul Laurence Dunbar, Jaki Shelton Green, Nikki Giovanni and Walt Whitman. These selections from various poets give students, whether teachers or young people, a chance to find their own level of engagement (i.e., the kind of issues they are willing to "act out" in public). The topics in my poetry collection include friendship, loneliness, racism, domestic abuse, women's rights, parents and children, and love. The wide range of poems, collected from books, former students, email messages, newspapers and poets who publish in journals and newsletters, allowed each participant the chance to find texts that fit his or her mood, experience and interest at the time of the workshop.

A favorite poem among the teachers was "My Mother's Hands" (author unknown):

Such beautiful, beautiful hands!
They're neither white nor small;
And you, I know, would scarcely think
That they are fair at all.
I've looked on hands whose form and hue
A sculptor's dream might be;
Yet are those aged, wrinkled hands
More beautiful to me.
Such beautiful, beautiful hands!
Though heart were weary and sad,
Those patient hands kept toiling on,
That the children might be glad.
I always weep, as, looking back
To childhood's distant day,
I think how those hands rested not

When mine were at their play.
Such beautiful, beautiful hands!
They're growing feeble now,
For time and pain have left their mark
On hands and heart and brow.
Alas! Alas! The nearing time,
When 'neath the daisies, out of sight,
These hands will folded be.
But on! This shadow-land,
Where all is bright and fair,
I know full well these dear old hands
Will palms of victory bear;
Where crystal streams through endless years
Flow over golden sands,
And where the old grow young again,
I'll clasp my mother's hands.

In the workshop I encouraged the group of five or six teachers to read poems like this one, drawing the stories, creating biographies about the lead characters in the poems they selected to work on, and writing editorials/songs/new poems/letters based on the characters described in the poems.

THE POETRY WORKSHOP

Presented in grades 6, 7 and 8. A five-week workshop schedule was used in the planning of the unit we called "Character Development through the Study of Text." We were open to change and responsive to the needs of the students in order to shape the poetry unit for their success in discovering character through text study (Team Meetings, April 2001).

THE FIVE BLOCKS OF THE WORKSHOP

The following outline presents the five blocks that I presented in my role as artist/collaborator, to Tracy, Lynn and Florence, the APAL team, at the first meeting on our Character Development Unit:

— Week 1: introduction to the poetry workshop

  • Students find poems from the collection in the library and look for clues to the character's "voice" in the text.
  • Teachers also choose a poem for their own exploration in the workshop.

— Week 2: practice with poems
  Activities lead students to

  • Identify with the character's "voice."

23

- Decide on the "point" of the poem, the story line (i.e., beginning, middle and end) and the attitude of the speaker.
- Write about the story told in the poem.

— Week 3: choosing the character

- Students find out about the poet and do research on the history, geography and events depicted in the poem.
- Students find a person or community that they can compare to the person/events in the poem.
- Students interview someone in the community who reminds them of the character. They write about the way that they identify with the character/community, do improvised scenes in class in character, and write "as if" they were the character (i.e., diary entries, newspaper editorials, letters to loved ones, etc.).

— Week 4: rehearsal of characters

- Students role play in pairs to develop the "voice" of the character, i.e., through the body language, the dialect, the clothing choices, etc.
- Teachers put characters in situations and let them improvise their reaction by speaking with someone whom they just met (i.e., on the phone, at the mall, on the street looking for a house they have never seen before, etc.).
- Students write about the experiences that came out of the improvisations based on character and situation.

— Week 5: presentation of the characters doing their poems

- Students review the research that led to the final choices, i.e., clothes, voice, dialect, historical perspective of the character, etc.
- The class looks at videotapes done during the journey to the final choices on character presentations to celebrate the journey.
- The class reviews interviews done with individuals in the community through scripted scenes that the students created.
- The class collects written documents from students in the voice of the character (i.e., letters, diary entries, newspaper articles, etc.). These will be collected and shared with other audiences.
- All "totems" that students and teachers produced as representations of their characters, i.e., paintings, new poetry, video presentations, music or art projects, are shown in the classrooms.

I also gave the teachers the following list of steps for analyzing a poem which were designed to help the students think independently and to give the teachers some choices in their development of each week's theme. This ensured that the team did not feel tied to the blocks outlined in the workshop plan.

STEPS TO ANALYZE A POEM

1. Read the title.
2. Read the poem.
3. Decide on the story line (i.e., beginning, middle and end).
4. What is the point of the poem?
5. What is the attitude of the speaker?
6. How do you relate to the attitude of the speaker?
7. Practice reading the poem out loud in the attitude you feel represents the character's feelings.
8. Listen to other people read the poem to you.
9. Write out the poem in your own handwriting.
10. What are some important features of the poem (i.e., repetition, length of the lines, order of the ideas, last word of each line (not sentence).
11. What points are important in the sequence of the story line (i.e., what happens in order of time/events)?
12. Memorize the poem.
13. Talk the poem "as if" you were someone else (i.e., your parent or least favorite teacher).
14. Use the poem as an excerpt of a conversation (i.e., pretend you are on the phone with a friend and you answer a question by using the poem you have memorized).
15. Listen to yourself performing the poem in character on a tape recording/video recording. Make changes to your presentation according to the effect that you are working to achieve.
16. Decide on the reason you need to say the poem, i.e., to convince, annoy, anger, show resentment or insult someone.
17. Decide on an event in your life that makes you feel like the character you are representing. How do you relate to the situation represented in the poem?
18. Reflect on the specific event or others like it before you present the poem each time.
    This exercise will help you to concentrate and present the poem in a convincing manner.
19. Reflect on your original "take" on the poem. How has it changed since you worked through these steps? How has it remained the same?
20. Enjoy sharing the poem in character with others!

STEPS TO PRESENTING A POEM: A CHEAT-SHEET FOR
STUDENTS AND TEACHERS

Step 1

Draw on the background experience of the students. This may be done by referencing the poems that the students read from the collection they looked at the day before. Students are then encouraged to talk about the stories that their poems represented.

Step 2

We get the students to focus on the attitudes/needs of each character by playing two games.

- Game 1: Pack a bag with objects that you believe your character would take on a journey (i.e., list the items, imagine the pieces and draw them, or prepare to tell your partner what things your character has in the bag and why they are there [Kaufman, 1999]).
- Game 2: Play Statues – each student finds a physical shape in which to stand/sit/lie that represents the attitude of the character (e.g., sad, angry, happy, expectant). Take Polaroid pictures of the students in their poses and then hang them on a wall for the viewing of the whole class. Students are encouraged to pick one of the poses that is different from their own character's body shape and draw it – even stick figures or three-dimensional models are acceptable. Students also have to talk to each other while holding the pose of their statue. This means that they have to adjust their voices and comments to match the physical reality of the statue (e.g., a sad pose produces a sad voice with many despondent comments about the topic that was presented to the character).

Step 3

Students experiment with their poems in different physical/vocal attitudes. This helps them realize the "point" of the poem and the possible ways in which the poet could be supported in making the story line clear. By "showing" how the character feels when he/she presents the lines in the poem, students have a chance to step outside their normal way of speaking and thinking (e.g., speaking in an excited voice or a slow, depressed tone).

Step 4

Students are encouraged to write about the story presented in their poem. The story may be told in another form (e.g., in the form of a letter, a newspaper editorial, an advertisement or a song). Each of these forms of the original story line should make the same point as the one made in the original poem. The students are also encouraged to share their new form of the story with the rest of the class in their character's voice.

Tracy's development of the four-step lesson plan provided a very useful tool for the other teachers and myself. The idea of scaffolding the workshop classes in "steps" allows teachers to feel safe within the creative environment. Because many teachers do not consider themselves "artists," they need the safety of the traditional language of lesson planning so that they can at least begin a class with an idea of what might take place in that session. If the class develops in a way that was unexpected, such as if one student were to create a character faster than the others, then the teacher may point that individual to another step to facilitate his or her creativity. In other words, the steps act as a safety net for the teachers. The safety net is a way of thinking about the class and how to facilitate student learning within each session.

THE PROCESS OF EACH CLASS AS A SERIES OF STEPS

Teachers should choose a vehicle (e.g., play a game like statues), that gives the students practical experience with the concept so that the teachers can see them "play" and "commit to the emotional reality" of the situation that the game demanded of them.

Each student

— shows that he or she understands key concepts, such as a character's attitudes and actions taught on the given day;
— sees the concept made personal through a demonstration, i.e., they can play statues and learn about physicalization;
— has a chance to practice and write about his or her experiences (e.g., play or draw a statue), and then write about what it was like talking as the character of the statue;
— begins practicing using the voices of the selected characters (e.g., a character based on Sojourner Truth should exhibit an authoritative voice), allowing the team to think in a sequential manner and to come up with age-appropriate activities for the three grade levels.

EXAMPLES

Florence chose to ask eighth grade students to bring in objects that represented their characters. Lynn asked students in the seventh grade to do a Venn diagram that helped them compare and contrast one character to another. They also compared features of their lives to those that they created for their character and thereby gained insight into the background of the life that they had imagined for each persona. The conversations that evolved from the activity in the eighth grade helped the students see that they could not do all poems in their own voice/attitude. Instead, they need to develop a menu of personae with different voices and physical characteristics, so that they can do convincing presentations of their characters.

LESSON PLAN FOR THE REHEARSAL OF CHARACTERS

Such terms as getting in character, motivation for speaking like the character and body language that creates the impression of the character, or physicalization, are all parts of the workshop experience. Next we used the boiler-plate agreed upon at the meeting preceding the rehearsal of the characters in the poem.

THE FOUR-PART LESSON PLAN

Step 1

Warm-up for the exercise on demonstrating the character in the poem:

- generate a list of characters;
- discuss the person/people in your life whom these characters remind you of;
- identify one character whom you want to study;
- list the reasons the character reminds you of that person and why.

Step 2

Show the character in the poem:

- Joanne presents her character from the autobiographical work "Between Me and the Lord," written and performed by her (Dowdy, 2000).
- Talk about the person whom you chose to model your character on.
- The teacher presents his or her poem.

Step 3: joint practice

We discuss the teacher's presentation with the class:

- We focus on "how students might put it together" (e.g., what they need to do to make the character credible).
- Students are invited to write a short description of why particular objects are in their bag.
- Students share their descriptions with the class.

Step 4: interviews in couples

Students talk as their characters based on their research leading up to this interview.

- Each person has four minutes to talk in character before he or she switches to let the other partner speak in character.

Talking in character
Talking in character became the touchstone of the poetry workshop. One student said that it was "very hard" to maintain the attitude of the character, especially if

you were doing the exercise on a day when you did not feel like being "happy or sad," or any other mood that the character represented. During the interviews of the characters, students realized they could not say things that were uninformed or not determined by a logical analysis of a character's background. For example, if they at first indicated that a person was 12 years old and an immigrant, they could not later say in the interview that the person was an American-born teenager who liked listening to Tupac Shakur's music.

Characters in interviews
. The "reality test" that the interview situations with characters provided brought home two ideas to the teachers and the students. First, they noted that while the character's reality is based to some degree on imagination, there must be logic in the way that the imagined reality is organized. In other words, if they want their audience to believe their character, they are responsible for building that credibility on a firm foundation of facts and history woven together into a believable story. The second idea was that the students became actors in this journey, working through the upper levels of Bloom's taxonomy, particularly analysis and synthesis, as they brought characters to life in the classroom (Bloom, 1971). This integration of arts in learning was the premise of the project. Those students who did not think deeply about their character's autobiography had a difficult time committing their imaginations to the process of the interviews.

EXAMPLE

When observing the teacher presenting her own character and then answering questions about the character's history, hobby and interests, it became patently clear that she did not expect the students to take the exercise as seriously as they did on that day. Having entered the world of play and the level of concentration that the students brought to the logic of that imaginary space, the teacher had to surrender her control of the situation as a "leader" and abide by the rules of the game. This was a new and "scary" experience for the teacher. She talked with me during a planning session about feeling "vulnerable" in front of the students and the fact that she did not think deeply about the way the character would draw on her own experience as a child before presenting her work. This was an important piece of the journey for both the teacher and the students, because it meant that they were beginning to see the importance of bringing life experience into the classroom (Ladson-Billings, 2002). The least well-served students now had a chance to better use their home experience in the classroom without it being subjected to criticism or being made invisible.

The students in Florence's class blossomed as they took ownership of their journey to discover the logic behind the stories that each poem represented. One student decided to interview a basketball player on the school team, because she believed that this player's personality represented the character in the poem. After her interview, she was able to imitate the player's voice and attitude, using these features to represent the character in her poem. The student showed the class a different side of her personality and impressed them with her ability to observe people and translate her findings into the work of character representation.

DISCUSSION

Poetry allows us to make an emotional connection with the characters represented in the stories that poets create. We may find ourselves relinquishing preconceived notions about another person, based on race, class or socio-economic status, because we come to identify with the personality we recognized in the poem. This empathy that is developed helps us to cut to the core of the human experience that is rendered through the lines on the page.

Adolescents are as vulnerable to the transforming experience as their teachers.

The subjects that are addressed in their choice of poetry can give them an opportunity to deal with their feelings and perception of situations in a safe environment. The poetry workshop that we sponsored also invited the students to experience the journey of making meaning through different forms of expression (e.g., drawing, acting, music, video presentations) to represent their understanding of the stories and the characters in the poems.

EXAMPLES

Tracy wrote early on in the workshop,

> Today we read "The Black Cat" excerpt ... we discussed vocabulary, meaning, attitude and the needs of the poet. Then I read the poem to them in "different voices" ... the kids were great, they were telling me ... "no, no, not like that ... that's too high a voice, go deeper, sound scarier, sound gruffer ... do a "proper" English accent ... that's too sing-songy ... more anger ...." We had FUN! ... They practice their own poems with each other next. This experience is really pushing me to do things differently ... I'm growing as a teacher because of this.

Lynn was relieved to report that

> Three boys in my class who have done almost NOTHING all year participated in Wednesday's statue exercise. Even if this doesn't raise anyone's test scores, that's enough for me. I had great success with statues the rest of the day, but I did not do Polaroids on my own. I simply extended the time we spent with statues and had some of the groups do a little performance by rotation through lines of their poems. It was really cool.

Tracy found that her experience with drawing could be used to encourage students to sketch characters and reflect on emotions and situations described in the poems. She also brought her fondness of music to the attention of the students when she dramatized her character and talked about the character's background. In her presentation during Week 4 of the workshop, she did her character's whole bag activity to the accompaniment of music. She danced during a part of the presentation, and the students seemed to transform from onlookers to fellow actors before our very eyes. I imagine that it looked to them as though their teacher had suddenly become more "human" – less of an authoritative figure who existed solely in order to give them directions – or part of a club that the students granted tremendous respect.

Lynn, a second teacher on the team, was able to focus on her interest in the community politics that were affecting the school system at the time of the project. By insisting that her students go out into the community and talk with people who reminded them of the characters that the poems helped them create, she made the language arts classroom a living experience and demonstrated the usefulness and power of language. The interviews that the students did with parents and professionals in their community not only provided an experience of preparing and performing live interviews but the opportunity to bring that information back so that their peers and teachers could benefit from the research. Mock interviews based on actual conversations with adults outside the classroom gave some students a forum in which to present themselves as adults with ample experience. They acted like people with personae completely different from their daily childhood masks. This transformation elicited a variety of responses from their classmates, including surprise, pride, a competitive spirit and respect for the kind of patience and collaboration that it takes for people to interview others. They also learned to cull the most important pieces of information from the discussion and figure out how to present these before an interested audience.

ACKNOWLEDGEMENTS

This Collaboration was made possible through the funding of the Atlanta Partnership for Arts in Learning (APAL), Alonzo A. Crim Center for Urban Educational Excellence, Georgia State University, Atlanta, Georgia, USA.

Note: [1] Dr Lisa Delpit, 1998, Principal Investigator of the UACC, personal conversation.

REFERENCES

Baker, J. (2002). Trilingualism. In L. Delpit & J. K. Dowdy (Eds.), *The skin that we speak: Thoughts on language and culture in the classroom*. New York: New Press.
Barbe, W. & Milone, M. N., Jr. (1980). Modality. *Instructor*, January, pp. 44–49.
Batker, C. (1998). 'Love me like I like to be': The sexual politics of Hurston's *Their eyes were watching God*, the classic blues, and the black women's club movement. *African American Review*, 32, 199–213.
Bloom, B. S. (1971). *Handbook on formative and summative evaluation of student learning*. New York: McGraw-Hill Book.
Cooper, A. J. (1892). *A voice from the South*. Xenia: Aldine Printing House.
Delpit, L. (2002). No kinda sense. In L. Delpit & J. K. Dowdy (Eds.), *The skin that we speak: Thoughts on language and culture in the classroom*. New York: New Press.

Delpit, L. (1995). *Other people's children: Cultural conflict in the classroom.* New York: New Press.

Dowdy, J. (1999). Becoming the poem: How poetry can facilitate working across differences in a classroom. In *The change agent, adult education for social justice: News, issues, and ideas.* New England: Literacy Resource Center.

Dowdy, J. K. (2000). *Between me and the Lord.* Clarkston, GA: Diaspora Productions.

Dowdy, J. K. (2002). Ovuh dyuh. In L. Delpit & J. K. Dowdy (Eds.), *The skin that we speak: Thoughts on language and culture in the classroom.* New York: New Press.

Dowdy, J. K, Givens, G., Murillo, E. G., Jr., Shenoy, D. & Villenas, S. (2000). Noises in the attic: The legacy of expectations in the academy. *International Journal of Qualitative Studies in Education, 13,* 429–446.

Edelman, M. W. (1984). *Black children in America. The state of Black America 1999.* Image Partners Custom Publishing/National Urban League.

Gardner, H. (1983). *Frames of mind.* New York: Basic Books.

Giddings, P. (1984). *When and where I enter: The impact of black women on race and sex in America.* New York: Bantam Books.

Harste, J. (1994). Visions of literacy. *Indiana Media Journal, 17*(1), 27–32.

Higginbotham, E. B. (1993). *Righteous discontent: The women's movement in the black Baptist church: 1880–1920.* Cambridge: Harvard University Press.

Kaufman, J. (1999). 'Hello, can you play?': Life's roles with puppet performances. In C. T. P. Diamond & C. A. Mullen (Eds.), *The postmodern educator: arts-based inquiries and teacher development.* New York: Peter Lang.

King, N. (1981). From literature to drama to life. In N. McCaslin (Ed.), *Children and drama.* New York: Longman.

Kozol, J., Wells. A. S., Delpit, L. D., Rose, M., Fruchter, N., Kohl, H., Meier, D. W., & Cole, R. (1997). Saving public education. *The Nation, 264*(6), 16–25.

Ladson-Billings, G. (2002). I ain't writin' nuttin': Permissions to fail and demands to succeed in urban classrooms. In L. Delpit & J. K. Dowdy (Eds.), *The skin that we speak: Thoughts on language and culture in the classroom.* New York: New Press.

Lederer, H. (1981). The play's the thing: The use of theater in language teaching. *Studies in Language Learning, 3,* 35–41.

Lerner, G. (Ed.) (1973). *Black women in white America: A documentary history.* New York: Random House.

Merriam-Webster's Collegiate Dictionary (1993). Springfield: Merriam-Webster.

Meyers, B., Dowdy, J., & Paterson, P. (2000). Finding the missing voices: Perspectives of the least visible families and their willingness and capacity for school involvement. *Current Issues in Middle Level Education, 7*(2), 59–79.

Obidah, J. E. (1999). First year documentation and evaluation report of the Urban Atlanta Coalition Compact. Atlanta: Georgia State University, Alonzo A. Crim Center for Educational Excellence.

Painter, N. I. (1996). *Sojourner truth: A life, a symbol.* New York: W. W. Norton & Co.

Perkins, L. M. (1980). Black women and the philosophy of 'race uplift' prior to emancipation, Working paper, ERIC Document Reproduction Service No. ED 221 444. Washington, DC: National Institute of Education (ED).

Reiff, J. C. (1992). *Learning styles: What research says to the teacher.* Washington, DC: National Education Association.

Robinson, L. C. (2001). France Ellen Watkins Harper. Available at http://www.africana.com/Articles/tt_289.htm

Short, K. G., Harste, J. C., & Burke, C. (1996). *Creating classrooms for authors and inquirers.* Portsmouth: Heinemann.

Woodson, C. G. (1994). *The mis-education of the Negro.* Newport News: United Brothers and Sisters Graphics and Printing.

JOANNE KILGOUR DOWDY

COMIC STRIPS ARE COMIC PLAYS

INTRODUCTION

This lesson shows the potential for using comic strips and comic books as a means to engage students in the literacy process. A connection is made to the current trend in films and animated television programming, showing how old comic book favorites have made it to the big screen. Student motivation reveals the popularity of reading comic books because the story lines are easily accessible and the artwork aids in comprehension. Bringing comic book pages to life through a workshop format is also presented.

STEPS TO THE WORKSHOP

Much like the first creators of the voice of "The Shadow" for *Detective Story* (Jones, 2004), students are encouraged to bring story characters to life with elements of voice, costume and movement. It is said of this fictive character that flamboyance, excess and shock values were the artistic features that the originator of this comic character represented to his audience. Cloaked in a black cape and hat slouched down as far as his nose, the slogan chosen for this mystery man was "The Shadow. He knows"(p. 74).

THE PROCESS

1. Share three samples of storyboards as they appear in comic strips, advertisements and student presentations of stories from books.
2. Have the group brainstorm about the features that they observe from the storyboard samples, i.e., the various frame sizes, the use of balloons for comments by characters, the use of bold colors for the frames, the use of space for different sized pictures of the characters.
3. Have small groups read selections from the many comic strips and allow them to decide on the ones that they want to use to create their feature film storyboard.
4. Share rolls of paper for tracing characters from the comic strips, as well as colored pencils for illustrating different scenes in the story line, and have the participants work on their storyboard drafts.
5. Share the drafts from each group of artists who have worked together.

J.K. Dowdy and S. Kaplan, Teaching Drama in the Classroom, 33–35.

6. Have the groups rehearse the scripts that they created to go with the frames in the storyboard so that there is a sound score to go with the pictures/frames.
7. Have the groups share their audio score with the rest of the group.
8. Discuss the ways in which writing-process methods were used in the creation of the storyboards.
9. Have participants share their ideas for using this method of writing in their own classrooms.

CONCLUSION

The inclusion of popular culture in the training of literacy students (Alvermann, Moon, & Hagood, 1999; Jacobs, 2007; Morrell, 2004; Xu, 2005; Yang, 2008) has been afoot as a teaching practice long enough for us to heed the signs of encouragement from our students. Meaningful interaction with the word and the world (Freire, 1972; Wallowitz, 2007) is not a new feature of our understanding of the way in which we can recruit members to the reading club. What we may be encouraged to do more often in our print-centered classrooms is provide a wider variety of prompts that lead students to read and write from a more personal and, therefore, meaning-filled perspective, so that they experience the value that formal literacy is touted to have for all those who engage in its use. As Botzakis (2009) reminds us, the growing line of converts to manga readers includes teenagers, and that represents a majority of young girls (Glazer, 2005). This would only continue in the line of development suggested by the already established work by Frey and Fisher (2004), Jacobs (2007) and Newkirk (2005) as we develop learning and positive engagement with our students' quest for ownership, friendship and meaning.

REFERENCES

Alvermann, D. E., Moon, J. S., & Hagood, M. C. (1999). *Popular culture in the classroom: Teaching and researching media literacy.* Newark, DE: International Reading Association.
Botzakis, S. (2009). Adult fans of comic books: What they get out of reading. *Journal of Adolescence & Adult Literacy, 53*(1), 50–59. DOI 10.1598/JAAL.53.15 DANIEL.
Freire, P. (1972). *Pedagogy of the Oppressed*, translated by M. B. Ramos. Harmondsworth: Penguin.
Frey, N. & Fisher, D. (2004). Using graphic novels, anime, and the Internet in an urban high school. *English Journal, 93*(3), 19–25. DOI 10.2307/4128804.
Glazer, S. (2005, September 18). Manga for girls. *The New York Times Book Review*, 16–17.
Jacobs, D. (2007). More than words: Comics as a means of teaching multiple literacies. *English Journal, 96*(3), 19–25.
Jones, G. (2004). *Men of tomorrow: Geeks, gangsters, and the birth of the comic book.* New York: Basic Books.
Morrell, E. (2004). *Linking literacy and popular culture: Finding connections for lifelong learning.* Norwood, MA: Christopher-Gordon.
Newkirk, J. (2005). It's not your grandpa's comic book anymore: A state initiative use of burgeoning graphic literature to motivate readers in Maryland and beyond. Paper presented at the International Reading Association 50th Annual Convention, San Antonio, TX.
Wallowitz, L. (2007). Disrupting the gaze that condemns: Applying a critical literacy perspective to Toni Morrison's The Bluest Eye. *The NERA Journal, 43*(2) 36–42.

Xu, S. H. (with Perkins, R. S., & Zunich, L. O.). (2005). *Trading cards to comic strips: Popular culture texts and literacy learning in grades K-8*. Newark: DE: International Reading Association.
Yang, G. (2008). Graphic novels in the classroom. *Language Arts, 85*(3), 185–192.

WILLIAM KIST

VIRTUAL ROLE-PLAYING

I must confess that I am one of those people for whom role-playing is a scary thing. When I was a child, I always dreaded the "audience participation" part of the program when my parents took me to a magic show or one of the animal acts at Sea World. And yet, as a teacher, I have seen the amazing power of drama in the classroom to bring concepts and texts alive for students who, perhaps, have difficulty conjuring up images from a printed page. Because I saw their great power, I continued to use very simple process drama activities in my classroom, all the while making sure there was a space for the "shy kid" or two who was always present and who always reminded me of myself.

Recently, while researching teachers who make use of what's known as "Web 2.0" in their classrooms (Kist, 2010), I have found that some teachers are using social networking platforms to set up virtual role-playing activities. These new media venues seem to capture the best of both worlds, keeping the creative play aspects of in-classroom drama activities, while allowing the more reserved students to do their "acting" in the (relative) privacy of the library, computer lab or their own homes. Also, these activities may spark some conversations about the nature of identity, which is probably a good thing for safety reasons in an age of online "profiles" that we all craft every day.

In my research, I have seen these interactive role-playing activities set up using three different platform: blogs, wikis and Nings. A blog is simply an online log ("Weblog") or journal designed for one person to share his or her thoughts with the world. A "wiki" (named originally for the Hawaiian word meaning "quick") is a virtual space for building collaborative texts online. The most famous example of a wiki is Wikipedia (www.wikipedia.org) in which people across the world collaborate on what are essentially encyclopedia articles about various topics. Finally, a few years ago, a website called Ning.com was created that allowed anyone to set up a social network that approximates Facebook or MySpace. One could set up a Ning for one's family, or club members, or around any activity through which people wanted to socially network. It allowed for discussions to form around any topic and for people to post pictures and various announcements. Nings were often used for online role-playing games. Unfortunately, Ning.com recently announced that it is going to begin charging people to use the web site (anywhere from $2.95 per month to $50 per month, based on the desired features). Due to this cost, I have decided to describe a virtual role-playing activity that is

J.K. Dowdy and S. Kaplan, Teaching Drama in the Classroom, 37–40.
© 2011. *Sense Publishers. All rights reserved.*

set up as a blog, because there are many sites that continue to host blogs for free. In addition, some school districts have their own in-house systems (known as "Intranets") that are ideal for hosting student blogs in a protected environment.

The first step in creating any kind of online role-playing activity is to find out what your district's policy is on having students keep blogs. Districts vary in their policies, and you may find any range of restrictions in place, so make sure to ask your principal or whoever is in charge of instructional technology in your district. Once you have determined that your district allows for student blogs, you can begin with the following steps:

1. Figure out the best venue for hosting your blog activity. The following sites are commonly used and are all free:

   Blogger (https://www.blogger.com/start)
   Blog.com (http://blog.com/)
   LiveJournal (www.livejournal.com)
   MSN Spaces (www.spaces.msn.com)
   Typepad (www.typepad.com)
   WordPress (www.wordpress.org)
   Yahoo 360 (www.360.yahoo.com)

2. Set up your own blog and practice blogging yourself for a few weeks, just to get used to the format of keeping a blog.

3. Go to Technorati (http://technorati.com/) which is an online repository of all blogs. Search for blogs that may exist dealing with the subject you are teaching. Assemble a list of these blogs and introduce them to students so that they can become familiar with the conventions of blogging. (See Kist, 2010, for general principles that can be set forth for students on how to be an ethical, responsible blogger.)

4. Decide what source text will be the springboard for your blogging activity. Obviously, the kinds of texts that lend themselves to this kind of activity are those in which there are characters that students can impersonate. These may be fiction or nonfiction texts.

5. If you teach multiple periods of the same course, consider whether you will set up one blogging project for all your classes together, or whether each class will have its own blogosphere. For example, if you are teaching *Lord of the Flies*, will there be one student impersonating Jack across all of your class periods, or will there be one student impersonating Jack in each of your class periods?

6. Start off with some simple prompts that may help your students be able to begin the role-play. Some simple prompt ideas are suggested in the box below.

Sample Role-Playing Prompts

1. In character, blog about something in your past that has motivated your actions. This experience could be something that is alluded to in the text or is imagined by you.
2. In character, create a blog post that essentially asks another character to explain his or her actions in the text. If you want, this post may be written in an angry fashion (if appropriate) or whatever other emotion suits the question.
3. In character, write a post that ties an event from the text to a historical event that forms the context of the story. Include as many historical "facts" as possible in your post so that it seems authentic.
4. In character, write a post that extends the story beyond the end as it exists in the text being read. This post essentially allows you to write a coda or an alternate ending to the story as it exists in the text.
5. In character, pick out a key event in the text and write a post that gets at your character's imagined feelings about that event. Get as much detail as you can about the event in your post, but, more importantly, explore how your character would react to this key event emotionally.
6. In character, write a post that talks about your character's favorite music, films, and/or books. Make it clear in the post what it is about these other texts that make them favorites of your character.

---

7. Develop (with or without student input) some criteria for the role-playing activity. Most teachers who do online role-playing are looking for some of the following to show up in the posts of the students:

   a) Do the blog postings capture the essence of the character being impersonated?
   b) Is there a certain number of references to the text being read: specific incidents mentioned or use of quotes?
   c) Is there some creativity and playfulness to the posts, or are students just repeating from the text verbatim? Are students taking what is in the source text and using imagination to take their characters to new levels (that are still true to their characters' identities)?
   d) Is the blogging medium being used to its fullest, with embedded hyperlinks and other multi-modal elements (graphics, music, etc.)?
   e) Is there some evidence that students are commenting on each other's postings in character? (This may be one of the most valuable parts of the assignment, as students are able to interact with each other via the comments they leave on each others' postings. It also allows for more interactivity than a traditional assignment in which students hand in their work to the teacher who is the only one who sees it.)

The last criterion above is probably the most important in making this activity come alive. If students are not commenting on each other's postings, then this activity runs the risk of just being a traditional kind of assignment in which the student is only writing for the teacher's benefit, in a two-way dialogue. It may be a good idea to give class time to allow students to read each other's postings and to comment on them. Once the commenting is started, it seems to gather momentum, as students can become addicted to seeing what new comment has been made, leading to further postings that clarify, leading to further comments, and so on. Along the way, it is a good idea to have some occasional in-class debriefing with the students, just to take the temperature of the class. Some possible debriefing questions and a timeline are included in the box below.

Debriefing Questions
(To be asked after one week of posting)

1. What are you learning about your character by blogging as him or her?
2. What are you learning about other characters by reading posts by your classmates?
3. What can be said in a blog format that can't be said in the text itself (if anything)?
4. What is to be gained by taking on the perspective of another person, even if fictional, in a role-playing activity? What does it feel like to take on a different identity?
5. How does this activity help or hinder involvement in the text we are reading?

Just as with any instructional activity, you will find that setting up blog role-playing has its advantages and disadvantages. I have found one main advantage is that it opens up the world of dramatic play for those shy students who don't feel comfortable with live role-playing. (I was one of those shy students myself!) After a week or so of blogging, you'll probably be amazed at the students who participate and those who don't. One disadvantage I'm finding in setting up activities like this is that some students are resistant to using technology. This may fly in the face of the common idea that all students born after 1990 were born as "digital natives" (Prensky, 2005). Some young people, interestingly, are expressing dismay at spending a lot of time in front of a computer screen. For those students, blogging may not help them to engage with their characters or the text. But that means that the face-to-face debriefing becomes even more important, and can open up a broader ongoing dialogue in your classroom that isn't text-specific: What are all the different ways we have today for expressing ourselves (both in and out of character), and how can we maximize the affordances that each of these media provides for communicating both our true and our made-up identities?

REFERENCES

Kist, W. (2010). *The socially networked classroom: Teaching in the new media age.* Thousand Oaks, CA: Corwin.
Prensky, M. (2005). Listen to the natives. *Educational Leadership, 63*(4), 8–13.

SANDY PERLMAN

PROPS, PHOTOS, AND CARTOONS AS PROMPTS

INTRODUCTION

Props work really well as prompts for creating characters. I always tend to use a lot of props, photos and cartoons. I cut out cartoons and photos, and I then ask students to pretend to be one of the people in a photo. I also ask them to use one prop as the trigger for creating one character. For example, I show them an object, like a flashlight, and then I ask them to write a monologue from the perspective of a person who sees the flashlight as an important thing in his or her life. The object chosen helps stimulate ideas and spark creativity.

We see about eight billion images a day, so when people say they have writer's block, I say, "I don't think so." What they have is self-censorship, and when a child says he can't write creatively, it just means that he thinks it's not going to be good enough. That's why with the first draft of anything, I tell students to free write. Free writing means without regard to grammar, spelling or rules. It's just write, write, write, write, write. This helps the students open up without worrying about doing it "right." They can concentrate on the voice of the character they are creating. The grammar and mechanics can always be polished later.

WHAT TO DO

1. The teacher collects a few objects for students to choose from for a writing prompt. Objects can range from household items like tools to more interesting items like pieces of jewelry.
2. The teacher instructs students to choose one object that they can create a character around. They should then write a monologue (7 to 12 sentences) from the first-person perspective of the character, showing attachment to the object in some way.
3. The teacher instructs students to focus only on the character's voice, not on grammar or mechanics, letting them know that they should just write without worry about rules.
4. The teacher allows time to do the writing.
5. The teacher asks students to perform their monologues as their characters. Another option is to pair them up and trade monologues so that they can direct someone else in performing his or her monologue.

Example: Prop is a stuffed animal.

Character's name is Maddy, that's my granddaughter's, one of my granddaughter's names. Mommy came home last night and I was so happy to see her. Daddy says she's been gone for ten years. All I know is I can't remember too much about her but my sister and I have wanted her home for so long. People say she left us to be with the, that other man, but I know she would never have gone with him on her own. I don't remember this but she says that I had put my little stuffed dog in her pocket the day the man took her. When she came home she had it with her. She told me that it was what she held on to all those years. She said she could feel close to, closer to my sister and me, just by holding it. Now she's home safe and sound and we are all one family again.

MUSIC

SANDRA GOLDEN

CREATING A MUSIC VIDEO
TO ENHANCE LEARNING

Today middle- and high-school teachers can use various methods and strategies to engage students in learning academic content topics. A lesson on creating a music video to demonstrate an understanding of an academic topic is one way to engage students in learning. Through this lesson, students are engaged and actively involved in reading, writing, viewing, acting, speaking and listening about a particular topic that invariably increases their depth of understanding of that topic. This lesson promotes cooperative learning and problem-solving opportunities. For instance, as a culminating activity in a literacy course I taught for pre-service content area teachers, they were assigned the task of presenting their understanding and benefits of literacy development in a dramatic form of their choice. Since this course focused on literacy development, the students were to use all they learned from watching videos, reading assignments, and group and class activities on literacy development to complete this assignment. These pre-service teachers created a five-minute music video "Just Read" in two weeks, whose theme was the importance and benefits of reading (see lyrics below). Through this activity, the students work cooperatively and collaboratively to form a concise and succinct understanding of reading.

Just Read
Written and Performed by Joshua Wade and Class of 2010
Reading in the Content Fields

Wake up in the morning and I grab a book
Borrowed it from the library; so, I ain't a crook
I really love to read because it makes me smart
I have so many books I can fill 10 shopping carts
Paragraphs on the page, page
Thousands of words like rage, rage
Look at this novel's age, age
I don't get mad because I'm smarter than you, you
There's so many books to choose, choose
Tryin' to get a little smarter!

J.K. Dowdy and S. Kaplan, Teaching Drama in the Classroom, 45–47.

Chorus
Just read and be free
You can think of what you want
Let your mind sail away
To a place like Vermont
Just read you and me
Nobody's gonna stop, no
(oh-whoa-oh-oh) (oh-whoa-oh-oh)

Ain't a word in any book I can't figure out
Storin' knowledge in my noggin is what I'm all about
Librarian tries to stop me that ain't nothing new
From checkin' out all the Dr. Seuss
Counting them fish like one, two
Seein' those colors like red, blue
Being small like Cindy Lou
Read, read till Grinch takes our books, books
Before the library closes down, down
Now, I gotta frown, frown
And, now I gotta frown

Chorus
J. K. you wrote some books
About a boy
Who had a scar
And stole our hearts
With your wand up
You stab me now
You got me reading
I don't know how
You taught me vowels,
Consonants too
From /A /to /E/
And /I/ /O/ /U?
Go get a book
Pick up a book
And, read a book
Now, the reading don't start till books open

ED 347 Ruff Readers (bark, bark)
What? Just Read!

STEPS IN WRITING, CREATING AND PRODUCING A MUSIC VIDEO

1. Students engage in a brainstorming activity to choose a topic/theme for the creation of a five-minute music video.
2. The instructor provides direction in the defining roles and responsibilities of students. For example, these may include production director, videographer, note-taker, costume and prop designer, lead singer, back-up singers, etc.
3. As a class students engage in the development and writing of the lyrics based on the main idea or theme of the topic.
4. Students create storyboards for the making of the video. Students brainstorm and write the scenes for the video.
5. Students provide music ideas for the video and then the class selects the most appropriate piece.
6. Students engage in discussions on class members' roles in the video, costumes, props and selecting film location.
7. Ample time should be provided for students to rehearse lyrics and scenes.
8. Lyrics are recorded with the music, the scenes are filmed, and then these are prepared for production with the use of movie-making software.

SUSAN V. IVERSON AND JENNIFER H. JAMES

SONGS OF CITIZENSHIP: THE USE OF MUSIC IN THE CLASSROOM

RATIONALE

Music can be introduced into the curriculum as a means to offer students alternative ways to engage content and express their understanding. Beyond being a curricular tool, however, we believe that music, as a form of media, is itself something to be thoughtfully considered for the messages it conveys and the ways it is used by individuals and groups of people to promote or protest particular ideas (Clay, 2006; Stovall, 2006). Such a study has potential to open students' eyes to new perspectives on, provide context for and ultimately to humanize the content under study (de Freitas, 2005; Hanley, 2007; Quaye & Harper, 2007).

Music is used for a variety of purposes. It is often used to create a mood or set a tone for audiences, as anyone who has ever watched a horror film or attended a pep rally can attest. It is used in advertising, where marketers develop catchy jingles or use music in order to capture specific consumer audiences. Music can be used to convey allegiance or loyalties, such as in anthems, battle songs or theme songs. During the 2008 presidential debates, both Barack Obama and John McCain used music as a way of characterizing their particular platforms. Obama's message of change and hope was captured in a compilation of songs including will.i.am's "Yes, We Can," which was played at his political rallies. McCain's theme song, "Raising McCain," sung by John Rich, was often interpreted as capturing the senator's maverick spirit. Throughout our history, music has been used to inspire action, to define communities and to resist oppression such as in African-American freedom songs and Vietnam-era protest songs.

Music is also used dramatically, most obviously as musical theatre and opera, to express beliefs, emotions, ideas and actions. Maus (1988), comparing a passage by Beethoven to a stage-play, illustrates how music-as-drama "presents a series of actions, performed by imaginary agents ... and [how] these actions are heard as taking place in the present" (p. 71). Maus anticipates his critics by qualifying that "actions in music are not as close to everyday actions as are the actions of nonmusical drama" (p. 71); yet, he argues we must focus less on the characters that might be agents of action and instead on music as "dramatic structure" that gives "a view to the action" (p. 72). In our own work with both undergraduate and graduate students from many different populations, we have used music in a variety of ways. To paraphrase Maus, the use of music in our teaching has

J.K. Dowdy and S. Kaplan, Teaching Drama in the Classroom, 49–54.

SUSAN V. IVERSON AND JENNIFER H. JAMES

provided the dramatic structure for students to represent civic actions. Here we describe our use of music to explore the concept of citizenship with students.

Because citizenship is a complex idea with which individuals and groups have had differing relationships over time, it offers a useful topic for interpretation and critical discussion. We have engaged first-year college students in studies of citizenship and their evolving roles as citizens of the university and larger community. We have similarly engaged upper-class students in studies of citizenship as they approach graduation and, for some, prepare to become public school teachers and civic educators. In each of these contexts, the use of music is adapted to meet the needs of individual students, but the core goals remain the same: (1) to introduce students to multiple perspectives on the content under study, (2) to offer context for conversations about complex ideas, and (3) to engage students in critical reflection on music's role in shaping and reflecting the ideas of individuals and groups of people. In what follows, we offer a brief description of two approaches we have developed to teach with music.

STEPS

Structured Approach

In this first version, we (as instructors) identify pieces of music representing various notions of citizenship. Examples include Toby Keith's "Red, White and Blue," John Mayer's "Waiting on the World to Change," Bob Marley's "War," Arrested Development's "Mr. Wendall," among many others. We distribute copies of the lyrics for each piece. We then play the songs, inviting students to jot down notes about the notions of citizenship they believe are captured in each. In particular, we ask students to think about the how the lyrics and musical composition work together to convey certain messages about appropriate citizenship. Once we have listened to the chosen songs, we invite students to share their thoughts about the individual pieces and then consider which song best represents their own views of citizenship and why.

Open Approach

Using a less structured, "open" approach, we ask students to identify a song or piece of music that they feel captures their own ideas about citizenship. Students are invited to bring in both the lyrics and a recording to share with the class. As each student makes his or her presentation to the group, the rest of the class is encouraged to carefully consider the piece presented and then respond to the following prompts:

- Identify one song (other than your own selection) that reflects your ideas about citizenship, and explain why.
- Indicate one song (other than your own selection) that offers a new perspective about citizenship that you hadn't considered before, and explain why.

50

In each of these approaches, music is employed as a means through which to consider competing ideas about citizenship – that, dramatically, might be considered plots through which students can view themselves as social actors (or note their civic absence). In the structured approach, students are presented with a variety of perspectives on citizenship and asked to grapple with them, eventually situating themselves among the ideas shared and explaining why. In the open approach, students are invited to bring in their own selections which they feel capture their personal ideas about citizenship and to share them with the class. Both approaches are intended to set the stage for critical discussion, in our case of citizenship. For our purposes, we strive to push students to consider why there are so many perspectives on what constitutes effective citizenship and how our individual biographies help to shape our views on the subject. However, these approaches have applications beyond a study of citizenship. Educators seeking to use music in their curriculum can adapt the above-described approaches to other topics and disciplines.

We offer a few considerations for educators seeking to adopt these approaches. With the structured approach, the instructor must familiarize him- or herself with musical selections related to the topic, in order to identify the songs in advance; with the open approach, the instructor serves as a facilitator for students' reflections on songs they have chosen. Instructors might find the open approach an easier transition to using music, since students' selections help the instructor build a music catalog. Coupling the open with the structured approach also holds potential to bridge any generational gaps that might exist, should the instructor's musical selections reflect a different era.

In addition to the two approaches described above, we suggest some other ways to incorporate music into one's teaching:

— Musical selections can be heard and watched through music videos. Instructors could tier the assignment by first reading lyrics, then hearing the song and finally watching the music video, with discussion following each activity.

— The teacher may assign students to perform selected songs. This idea was inspired by one student who requested to bring his guitar and play his selection. While some students might argue their limited musical talents, it is an option for those with creative inclination – or at least for the exhibitionists.

— Students may be arranged in small groups with peers and invited to share reactions to each other's selections, pose questions about music and solicit feedback from group members.

— Instructors can use music as entrée to a lesson or to elicit alternative thinking about a subject. For instance, in a discussion with graduate students about designing educational programs to raise awareness about social issues, students focused largely on lecture-based delivery mechanisms. After being introduced to a selection by the Sinikithemba Choir, a group of HIV infected Zulu men and women from South Africa who, through the choir, gain support and raise awareness and funds, the students' thinking creatively shifted to educational alternatives.

Through music, students can employ perspective taking, critical thinking and problem solving, as well as engage in meaningful discussion about how we perform social roles. Music in our teaching is a tool through which students may be receptive to concepts that were initially viewed as uninteresting. Music can be provocative and informing, oppositional and unifying; it has the potential to give voice to (disenfranchised) experiences and to elicit critical consciousness (de Freitas, 2005; Hanley, 2007).

SAMPLES

In this section, we provide illustrations of some of the powerful discussions and learning that have grown out of our use of such methods.

Using the structured approach, students in a social studies methods course for pre-service primary educators read lyrics and listened to songs ranging from Toby Keith's "Courtesy of the Red, White and Blue" to Country Joe and the Fish's "Feeling like I'm Fixing to Die Rag." Students, responding to a prompt to identify which song resonated most with their views on citizenship, largely pointed to John Mayer's "Waiting on the World to Change":

> Now we see everything that's going wrong
> With the world and those who lead it
> We just feel like we don't have the means
> To rise above and beat it
> So we keep waiting
> Waiting on the world to change

Students[1] reflected:

> I believe these songs really inform us of what is really happening in the world, especially the John Mayer song because that is what is happening. We need to take a stand. (Mark)

> I agree with what [John Mayer] is saying. I do think that *many* people are just sitting back waiting for someone else to do something to change the world. (Alice)

> The song by John Mayer was kind of a wake-up call. I've listened to it a thousand times but never actually understood what he was saying. (Leslie)

> John Mayer's song really got me thinking. I need to be more of a change; it's just hard and I don't know where to start. (Jayme)

---

[1] Pseudonyms are used for students' statements.

I agree; we are waiting for change. Most of us don't take action or didn't really know how, so we wait for someone else or something to make a difference, a change. But we can't let this keep happening. We need to stand up for ourselves and beliefs, rights, etc. (Kirsten)

Using the open approach in a seminar on citizenship, students brought many songs, ranging from Nas' "I can" to Three Doors Down's "Citizen Soldier," from Pink's "Dear Mr. President" to Marvin Gaye's "What's going on?" When asked to complete an in-class writing assignment indicating a song that reflected their ideas or that offers a new perspective about citizenship, many students pointed to the artist will.i.am's "Yes, We Can," which we will use to illustrate this approach. Selected lyrics from this song, inspired by a speech delivered by Barack Obama, assert the following:

We know the battle ahead will be long
But always remember that no matter
What obstacles stand in our way
Nothing can stand in the way of the power
Of millions of voices calling for change.

Students, reflecting on these lyrics, wrote

It shows that there is something that can unite us on common ground. (Jonathan)

We can change if we put our mind to it. (Kaymi)

Speaks about how we can repair this world and what we can do about it – justice, equality, and change. (Mark)

We can do anything we want, no matter the issue or problem. (Sally)

Students, when asked to reflect on the value of this assignment – specifically the use of music to elicit discussion about citizenship – offered affirmations on how their thinking was influenced.

This assignment gave me different ideas on citizenship. (Catherine)

I thought this was a fun assignment. While I was looking for songs, I thought [about what] citizenship was. (Natalie)

I thought it was cool that we got to discuss songs that relate to us. It makes the class more real. (Peter)

I really liked the music and citizenship homework. ... It was interesting to hear other students' music [and how] everyone has a different definition of citizenship. (Kelly)

Their statements and insights further illuminate, and fuel more ideas about, the power of and potential for the use of music in teaching.

REFERENCES

Clay, A. (2006). All I need is one mic: Mobilizing youth for social change in the post-civil rights era. *Social Justice, 33*(2), 105–121.

de Freitas, E. (2005). Pre-service teachers and the re-inscription of whiteness: Disrupting dominant cultural codes through textual analysis. *Teaching Education, 16*(2), 151–164.

Hanley, M. S. (2007). Old school crossings: Hip hop in teacher education and beyond. *New Directions for Adult and Continuing Education, 115,* 35–44.

Maus, F. E. (1988). Music as drama. *Music Theory Spectrum, 10* (Spring), 56–73.

Quaye, S. J. & Harper, S. R. (2007). Faculty accountability for culturally inclusive pedagogy and curricula. *Liberal Education, 93*(3), 32–39.

Stovall, D. (2006). We can relate: Hip-hop culture, critical pedagogy, and the secondary classroom. *Urban Education, 41*(6), 585–602.

DIANA L. AWAD SCROCCO

USING MUSIC AS A THEME IN AN AURAL PROJECT IN A COLLEGE WRITING COURSE

RATIONALE

This four-week project was conducted in the context of a semester-long composition course focusing on the theme of music. The students were college freshmen from various disciplines and with various experiences who used software to produce multimodal projects. In the first project of the course students composed narratives connecting events in their lives to a specific song, and in the second project they interviewed a peer and produced a visual project presenting the way music can be used to tell another person's story. Students used their own opinion and outside credible popular sources to assert their perception of the music and songs that characterize their generation or subculture. Then students dramatized their argument in an aural essay, using their own narration, music, media interviews and sound clips to demonstrate why specific music represents their generation or subculture.

The Assignment

In this project you will consider your generation or subculture's musical identity. Consider what name might be given to your generation/subculture, what genre of music seems most popular to people in your age group or in your subculture, what songs and lyrics might emerge from your era as "classics" and how music videos reflect your age group or subculture. You will write a *3–4 page script* defending your impression of your generation/subculture's musical identity by using *examples* from musical texts and *one or more popular source citations*. Next you will dramatize parts of your argument by integrating your script with songs and sound effects into a *5–7 minute aural essay*.

WHAT TO DO

1. Require students to free-write about the music they think represents their generation or subculture by naming, explaining and providing examples of specific music and artists.
2. Listen to a professional radio show (available through "This American Life") and require students to create sound maps of the radio show; sound maps should diagram how music, narration and sounds have been layered in the show to create a specific dramatic effect.

J.K. Dowdy and S. Kaplan, Teaching Drama in the Classroom, 55–57.

Example of part of a sound map:

Narrator introduces the show and the topic: talking about different types of maps	Narrator introduces a cartographer with whom he'll talk	Transitional classical music in forefront
Slow, subtle, classical music plays in background	Sound effects from NYC streets in background	No speaking

3. Form groups and discuss how the narrator of the radio show dramatizes her or his main arguments through variations in intonation, volume, rhythm, pitch, different background music, pausing, integration of others' voices, etc. Talk about the ways that mood and emotion are generated through these and other variations in sound effects.

4. In groups discuss how the director creates theatrical effects in each segment of the show:

   a) How does the narrator draw the reader in during the *introduction* through dramatic effects? (humorous or riveting story, startling question, unexpected statement, long pause, sound effects, music, emotional medley, quotation, greeting)

   b) How do the narrator's tone, rhythm, pitch, rate and volume infuse emotions into the stories and arguments? What main sentiments emerge as the narrator speaks?

   c) How does emotion emerge in the *body* of the radio show? (examples/stories/music)

   d) How do these examples, stories and music create dramatic effects in the show? (context/emphasis/contrast/clarification/example)

   e) What generates the emotional effect in the *conclusion* of this radio show? (funny or depressing anecdote, suggestions for future action, list of thought-provoking questions, description of consequences, summary, emotive suggestion for activism).

5. During a workshop, allow students to search the Web for songs, media interviews and other sound clips that demonstrate music/artists that they believe define their generation.

6. At home, require students to use their free writing to create a script for the narration of their argument.

7. In class, ask students to pair off and practice performing the dramatic effects of their script using some of the techniques in 4a-e above. Encourage them to try a couple of different strategies for each major section of their script (introduction, body, conclusion) and encourage their partners to take notes on which techniques work better than others.

8. In groups, ask students to produce sound maps of their own aural essays by deciding how to layer their scripts, songs, media interviews, sound clips

and others' voices to dramatize their argument about the music defining their generation or subculture.

9. At home, ask students to use sound-editing software (e.g., Audacity) to record their aural essay using their script, the sound files they collected in class and their sound maps.

10. In class, require students to workshop drafts of their sound essays by critiquing each other's aural essay: introduction, body and conclusion.

11. Once students have revised and edited their sound essays, have them present their projects in class.

12. Ask all students to take notes on the strengths and limitations of their peers' sound essays and provide each presenter with feedback about the dramatization of the argument about her or his musical generation or subculture.

JOANNE KILGOUR DOWDY

MUSIC AND DRAMATIC PLAY

READING THE WORLD

In the young adult novel *What Happened to Lani Garver* (2004), the young Lani explains to his new friend, Claire, that "when people realize you can see past their eyes and into their heads … they don't take kindly to that," since no one would like it much if someone "started looking inside your head at your hidden garbage" (p. 48). Lani explains to Claire that people like her who are "most afraid of their own thoughts spend half their lives with their arms crossed" and that she could do herself a great favor by finding a psychiatrist. When Claire lowers her body from Lani's direct gaze and avoids eye contact with him, he explains to her that she has just performed another version of the "defensive stance" (p. 49).

This ability to read people and understand the contexts in which they express their choices is one of the founts of experience that young people bring to learning sites. Any teacher able to identify this talent and use it to bridge students' journeys to new experiences can facilitate it by adding different kinds of expertise to their skills in reading as an active process (Brooks & Brooks, 1993; Freire & Macedo, 1987; Langer, 1992; Probst, 1988; Rosenblatt, 1938). Such an approach to reading and communicating effectively supports the idea that Wallowitz (2007) described in her observation that education can serve more interests than simply being a means to socialize and control students, leaving the poor, minority and learning disabled in the margins.

MUSIC SCORES AS PROMPTS

I have a selection of music scores that have been collected over the years. They include scores by J. Rosamund Johnson, George Harrison, Claude-Michel Schonberg, Arthur Herzog and Billie Holiday, and Keith Christopher. Students are also encouraged to find music scores from musicals such as *Hair* (Ragni & Rado, 1967), which has recently made a comeback as a successful Broadway show. The lyrics in this show help students understand the way that history was documented in a non-print communication system. My student teachers were surprised to find a wealth of social commentary in the way that the Vietnam War was used as background for the social upheaval that was going on in the country at the time that the musical was written. The new teachers also find other themes and events described in lyrics as they research the topics that they have to teach in their

J.K. Dowdy and S. Kaplan, Teaching Drama in the Classroom, 59–62.
© 2011. *Sense Publishers. All rights reserved.*

content areas. Many websites offer choices for the study of physical education, social studies, art, business, music and health education.

The students are invited to work in pairs or trios as they scan pages with musical notation. They must take note of the patterns that they observe and make some sense of the message that the patterns are communicating. For example, if a page has more single notes appearing together more often than the series of notes joined together, there may be a meaning behind that order of presentation. Students create a story grammar with beginning, middle, and end, which they feel represents the message being communicated by the pattern of the symbols, or notes on the page, that they have to study.

In one workshop a duet working together on a page of the score decided that they had far more small symbols standing alongside each other than any other notes on the page. They created a story about the relationship between this long line of single notes that were more powerful and the two fat notes that were hooked together at the bottom. They were asked, "Who are you and what are you doing here?" In response, they told a story about being crowded into a housing area where they did not have much room to do anything outside their small apartments. The feeling they got from watching all those quarter notes, lonely figures, lined up one after another on the page, was claustrophobic, as though they needed to break out from the uniform lines that oppressed them on the page. Each of the characters depicted had a story that matched the general description of people striving to overcome their immediate environment.

After the two students stood in a tableau, representing one person trying to get away from the other, they were invited to start improvising lines in a conversation. Their dialogue represented the struggle between two people who were having an intense argument. One person was insisting that the other one stay in the place where they were having the conversation. The argument became more intense as the actors began to make physical actions that demonstrated their conflict. We soon asked them to freeze in the tableau that first initiated the conversation in the improvised scene.

The challenge of this part of the workshop is to keep students focused on the attitude that the characters present – that is, angry, happy, sad, reluctant, bossy – while they make up lines to advance a conversation with another character. When a character has to initiate a conversation or respond to another person in the chosen attitude, he or she may not switch out of that persona. The idea is to respond to the input in the conversation while maintaining the belief that "I am that attitude." This requires the students to keep their body and voice in a position different from normal, and advance both the conversation and the mood of the improvised situation at the same time.

THE WORKSHOP: INTO THE PICTURE

1. Participants choose a character from the image presented.
2. Bullet-list the "character" that you can pick out, that is, people, things, colors, setting.

3. Choose one character in the image and do a Character Story for that individual or object.
4. In groups the participants decide how to represent the image in which their character exists, as a tableau.
5. Groups look at other groups' pictures.
6. Groups create a character sketch for each character in the picture. (See *Cycle of the Character's Story* below for a complete description of the process). Answering the questions, who, what, when, where and why, helps each person write a first-person narrative about the character that he or she represents in the picture.
7. Share each person's character description in the group.
8. Taking places in the tableau again, the characters answer two questions when the teacher touches them on the shoulder: (1) Who are you? and (2) What are you doing here? The character answers based on the created narrative.
9. Groups discuss the actual events that led to the situation captured by the image, including a beginning, middle and end, up to the scene where the tableau comes to life. Each character should have something to say, or a reaction, when the scene is presented for the rest of the class.
10. Review the process of arriving at the scene created for the group in the tableau: (a) What writing steps did the group follow? (b) How does this process support literacy development? (c) How can it be used in different content areas to support the Department of Education's content standards for teaching? (d) What materials are necessary for the successful completion of the exercise in any classroom?

The tableau enables students to create with others, and because they have written the narrative as a part of the research on the character they represent, each individual can be spontaneous about sharing the story that has led to the point in life where we meet him or her in the scene. This ensures that all the students in the class ask each character about his or her purpose for being in the scene. Students have a chance to use their imagination within the context of the story that the group is representing. Those who are watching the act of invention take place are learning about the way in which story grammar works (Montague, Maddux, & Dereshiwsky, 1990).

CYCLE OF THE CHARACTER'S STORY

In order to create a character's history, the class is invited to go through a series of creative writing exercises, according to the following directions:

1. Choose a character from the image that you are using as a prompt.
2. Decide on a crisis event or wounding, or a learning or discovery event that your character experiences in the course of his or her life. For example, if your character has had a parent die, that is considered a wounding event. Try to fill in as many details as possible about the critical event that the character has experienced.

3. Finally, create a scenario in your mind's eye about the way in which the critical incident is now applied to the character's life, that is, how does he or she use the learning or discovery to resolve new crises? Write as much as you can about this learning and its application to the character's life (Personal conversation, Jacqueline Peck, March 21, 2008).

4. Use a book with character sketches, or comic books or graphic novels with clear characters, so you can pick a face that matches the person you have created and trace the outline of the image. You may use the hair from one portrait, the expression from another, and the shape of the eyes and nose from yet another drawing in any magazine, comic book, newspaper comic strip or children's coloring book.

REFERENCES

Brooks, J. G. & Brooks, M. G. (1993). *In search of understanding: The case for constructivist classrooms*. Alexandria: ASCD.

Freire, P., & Macedo, D. (1987). *Literacy: Reading the word and the world*. New York: Bergin and Garvey.

Langer, J. A. (1992). *Literature instruction: A focus on student response*. Urbana: NCTE.

Plum-Ucci, C. (2004). *What happened to Lani Garver*. New York: Harcourt.

Probst, R. E. (1988). *Response and analysis: Teaching literature in junior and senior high school*. Portsmouth: Boynton/Cook.

Ragni & Rado (1967). *Hair*. Broadway musical score.

Rosenblatt, L. (1938). *Literature as exploration*. New York: Appleton-Century.

Wallowitz, L. (2007). Disrupting the gaze that condemns: Applying a critical literacy perspective to Toni Morrison's the Bluest Eye. *The NERA Journal, 43*(2), 36–42.

TERRY L. BOYARSKY

USING MUSIC AND MOVEMENT TO DEVELOP CHARACTER AND ILLUSTRATE CONFLICT RESOLUTION

This workshop was created to address some of the dynamics of music and movement that also apply to the theater. As a performing musician, singer and dancer, my teaching philosophy starts with deep experience. Later, we can (and will) discuss, notate, analyze, compare and share. Theater is an interesting art form because it shares aspects with literature and visual art, and contains facets of all the other performance arts – voice, movement and music.

I was asked to create a workshop that gets students moving and making music. I took several ideas from theater (sequence, character development and resolving conflict) and showed how these concepts also exist in movement and music.

Paying attention is the most important element in teaching; it is also the most important element in performance where perhaps it can be called *listening*. The best way to develop attention is to create games where mind, body, emotion and spirit all work together. They have to be fun, intriguing, challenging and paced in response to the specific group. The exercises were set up as interlocking puzzle parts which involve and engage students immediately. We started with rhythmic and musical exercises to warm up the mind, ear and body before we did the following explorations. Here's how we worked:

1. Improvisation to develop character

Moods: I asked for volunteers to create four statues, each representing a contrasting feeling: *sad*, *mad*, *glad*, *scared*. Each statue must include posture, gesture, facial expression. The energy of each statue must relate to that state of emotion.

Form a circle: One by one and in the correct order (1. sad, 2. mad, 3. glad, 4. scared), each person takes the statue and holds it (freezes). I played the drum so the student can "meet" the beat, take the statue exactly at that moment, trying to truly inhabit each mood. The drummer can play big beats or set up a meter, such as 4/4, and the statue can be taken on the downbeat (the first of 4 beats).

"*Soundscapes*": Students draw a symbol to represent each mood, and the class chooses a conductor who points to each symbol. Students use their voices to "paint" the sound of this mood. The conductor can move from symbol to symbol, in any order, at any speed, to create a new piece.

J.K. Dowdy and S. Kaplan, Teaching Drama in the Classroom, 63–65.

Slow motion: Using both sound and statue, students morph from one to the next in eight beats. The class can predetermine the order or choose a conductor to indicate the sequence. The class plays with and explores all these elements of posture, mood, sound and movement.

2. Interacting characters

Contrasting rhythms: Students learn these two contrasting and interlocking rhythms and practice saying them, clapping them, stepping them. They step the exact rhythm across the floor. It is very important that they step lightly and flowingly and not drum or stomp the feet into the floor. They create their own body percussion version (using snaps, claps, patches and stamps) of each. They must make sure they contrast, for example, by using snaps and claps for the first one, pats and stamps for the second.

a) *"Class room drama"* (step backwards) – ♩ ♩ ♪♩.

b) *"Music and movement"* (step forwards) – ♪♩♪ ♩ ♩

Students play with the dynamics (volume) and tempo (speed) of the rhythms. The class is divided in half. One half does one rhythm, while the other half does the other, one after the other and then simultaneously. Students are told, "Listen! Feel the energies and qualities in your voice and body."

Interacting: Students choose partners and decide who goes first. They alternate taking the four mood statues. They must decide on their meter, tempo, sequence of moods and how long they will hold the statues. They may experiment with trios and quartets and with floor space and levels (high, medium, low).

Person A	Person B	Person A	Person B
Statue 1	Statue 2	Statue 3	Statue 4

As students explore, they start to notice the other person and begin responding to exactly what they see and feel in the other person. They add voice, as in the Soundscapes above.

3. Resolving conflict

Brainstorm: Students create a cast of four characters, each having a predominant mood, and imagine a story line behind each character. What words would they use to describe these characters? Students create a word wall of adjectives for each character and give him or her a name.

For example, "Zhenya" – short, shy, ashamed, reticent, servile, simple.

Ostinato: Students create a short chant that describes their character succinctly. This is the basis for the rhythmic motif which is repeated for each character (an ostinato). They must make decisions about the timbre of the voice: will it be high? low? growly? soft? accented?

For example, Zhenya speaking in the first person: "I am afraid I'm shy."

His rhythmic signature (ostinato) would be ‖ ♩ ♪. ♪ ♪♪ ♩ ‖

Students chant each character's ostinato four times in a row. They use tone of voice, facial expression, posture and gesture to strengthen the entire image of the character Zhenya. They move across the floor as Zhenya would move.

Musical/Movement conflict: Students then pick some of the characters to have a conversation in movement, body percussion (using the rhythmic ostinato) or chant. They experiment and observe, trying different combinations of people, using duos and trios, in order to interact with just body movement and then with just tone of voice, no words (vocables). Students discuss different ways to resolve a conflict: Will the partners overpower each other? Blend with each other? accept each other? Find ways to coexist? Negate each other?

ADAPTING LITERATURE

KAREN GREENE SEIPERT

DEVELOPING LITERATURE THROUGH DRAMA

RATIONALE

I have taught English Literature at both the university and high school levels. Throughout my teaching career, I have noticed that my students respond to literature in different ways, according to their personal literacy levels. My literature students worked through the reading and writing assignments with relative ease, while the less literate ones struggled through the readings. The same students who displayed difficulty reading also had trouble keeping up with their more literate classmates in the writing tasks that required reading comprehension in order to complete literary analysis essays. I also discovered that my most creative literary assignments were often the ones that evoked the most enthusiastic student responses, especially from those students with reading comprehension problems. Through trial and error, I found that my students' reading comprehension reached its peak when I required the students to "act out" the readings, either through dramatic readings or scene performances.

As an instructor who has always enjoyed student-centered classrooms with full class participation, I believe that drama is the perfect way to develop literature. Students enjoy the interaction with the text while becoming excited by the feelings of ownership in their own learning that dramatic performance affords them. My students became so interested in the dramatic exercises that they eagerly stayed motivated and on-task with the assignments. The literature lessons were created to reinforce the students' knowledge of the use of literary and dramatic elements in works of literature.

WHAT TO DO

- Select collaborative groups.
- Select literary piece for adaptation.
- Read the literary piece.
- Discuss the adaptation issues:
  1. Setting – can we recreate the setting in an effective way?
  2. Plot – does the plot lend itself to being rewritten for performance?
  3. Costumes – do we need or desire them during performance?
  4. Historical accuracy – how far, if at all, should we compromise the historical facts?

J.K. Dowdy and S. Kaplan, Teaching Drama in the Classroom, 69–70.

5. Props – are they affordable and feasible give the limitations of the classroom?
6. Characters – should the same ones be used or should we conglomerate some of them?
7. Author's intent – can we rewrite without compromising the integrity of the piece?
8. Time frame – how much to rewrite and perform given the class' time constraints?
9. Language – how adaptable is the author's language to the class' purpose?

– Assign individual duties.
– Create the script.
– Group member input and revisions.
– Practice.
– Performance.
– Evaluate the group, class and instructor.

CARIE CSEAK GREENE

MIME IT

RATIONALE

Mime It helps students review characters, setting, practice the sequencing of the text, and bring literature to life. It also aids in the development of creativity, imagination, inventiveness, cooperative learning, teamwork collaboration, democratic participation and social development. The students select a scene from the assigned literature to mime. No scenes should be repeated. It is better *not* to repeat scenes so that the whole story may be captured during the mimes. Any text can be adapted to *Mime It*, although the educator should make sure that enough scenes are available for the students to mime. For this reason the teacher may want to wait until several chapters of a book are read, then inform the class that they may select from the several chapters for their scenes. The actors and actresses of the scenes are not allowed to talk during their performance, which will be mimed in front of the class.

WHAT TO DO

1. Assign literature for students to read with enough live action for pantomime. If the students have not participated in pantomime previously, the teacher may want to mime an act (not from the text), such as baking a cake or changing a tire, to help the students to understand the concept of pantomime.
2. Allow students to form their own cooperative learning groups or draw students' names out of a box to form the groups. Each educator should know which option will work best for her/his students. The number of students in the groups should be determined by the literature and the teacher.
3. Students need to discuss the story in their group, then work together to decide which scene in the text they would like to mime. Allowing the members of the groups to define their own scene helps the students develop their knowledge of the literature and how that literature is divided into scenes. The participants should develop their suggestions and vote on which suggestion is preferred by the majority in their group, thus participating in democratic selection. Each group needs to do this procedure very quietly so that the other learning groups will not be able to hear its scene choice, because the other students will be in competition to identify which scene is being presented.

J.K. Dowdy and S. Kaplan, Teaching Drama in the Classroom, 71–73.

4. A student in each group should write down the page numbers of their chosen scene on a paper and give the note to the teacher. The first group that gives the page numbers to the teacher will be permitted to mime that scene.

5. Students should discuss their strategies and plan how they will mime the scene from the story. The learning groups need to quietly practice their scenes several times until they are ready to perform their acts in front of their audience.

6. A student from each group should write on a piece of paper, called a completion slip, that they are prepared to perform their pantomime and give the completion slip to the teacher. The groups will stage their productions in the same order in which they finished their rehearsals and in the order that the instructor received their completion slips.

7. After the teacher receives the group's rehearsal completion slip, the learning group may use any of the art supplies in the art corner to make scenery or props for their performance. Any available articles, such as books, pencils, paper, etc., may be used in the pantomimes. If a group takes too long to rehearse its scene, it may not have sufficient time to make props or scenery. The teacher should explain that it is acceptable to have no scenery or props, since most mimes use neither.

8. All groups present their pantomimes to their classmates without telling which scene they are performing. Their peers try to guess which scene of the story the group is performing.

9. After a couple of groups have presented their pantomime, the entire class can make a sequence diagram on the white board or a large, poster-sized paper to place the scenes of the literature in order. Subsequently, each scene from the pantomimes can be added to the sequence diagram to provide a more comprehensive understanding of the text.

SAMPLES

Mime It works well with novels and stories with a lot of action and many characters. However, I have also used it with books that have a small number of characters. When there are few characters, the teacher should advise students that they may be the pets in the stories or inanimate objects. I once had a group of students who portrayed a scene in which there were many bubbles. Several students made a circle shape with their hands to represent the bubbles and proceeded to move around the classroom with their "bubbles" in a floating manner to represent the bubbles hovering in the air. Therefore, teachers should inform students that they may illustrate inanimate objects by taking on the shape of the object, as one of my students did when he "became" a car on his knees and hands. Another student climbed on his back and mimed a steering wheel which helped display the "driver" turning corners.

Brave New World (1932/2006) by Aldous Huxley is the type of book with which *Mime It* works well. The beginning of the second chapter of *Brave New*

World is a good example of an appropriate scene for students to mime. In this scene there are numerous characters who are active. The Director of the Central London Hatchery and Conditioning Centre guides a group of students around the Infant Nurseries and Neo-Pavlovian Conditioning Rooms. In the rooms are a half-dozen nurses, who, at the Director's command, leave the room and return with several eight-month-old babies. They allow the babies to crawl on the floor toward beautiful roses and numerous books. One nurse is standing by a lever which she pulls forcefully to produce an electrical shock. After she pulls the lever, the babies are violently shocked, causing their bodies to twitch and stiffen; "their limbs moved jerkily as if to the tug of unseen wires" (Huxley, 1932/2006, p. 21).

Although *Brave New World* (1932/2006) is a perfect example of how *Mime It* can be used, my students came up with many surprising pantomimes for books with fewer characters and less action. I observed that the more frequently I allowed the students to mime literature, the more they became proficient at miming and, therefore, more creative and inventive. In addition, students enjoyed miming, and many requested that we participate in pantomime more often.

REFERENCES

Huxley, A. (1932/2006). *Brave New World.* New York: HarperCollins.

JACLYN CONSILIO

LESSON: CREATING YOUR OWN CANTERBURY TALE

Time Frame: 8 Days
Grade: 11th

THE RATIONALE

This workshop was developed for students to be able to create iambic pentame-
ter poetry and to realize just how difficult it can be. By learning to analyze the
historical and social context from Chaucer's time and adapt it to create a modern
version, students will be bale to make Chaucer's tales relevant to their personal
lives. Students will reflect on aspects of today's middle class society. His tales are
still popular today and students should have an understanding of why they are still
entertaining.

Many students have composed poems in English class and turned these in
and that was it; with this project students are able to "give life" to their tale by
recording it as an audio file in the program Audacity. Students will record their
tale in the true voice of their character while adding sound effects and music to
bring their tale to life. From here, they turn their tales into MP3s and Podcasts
and can share them with hundreds and thousands of people. Students learn how
to incorporate technology and digital tools to promote learning and creativity.
Students end up with a final product they are proud of and are able to share
literally across the world.

ACTIVITIES

1. After reading *The Canterbury Tales*, students will participate in a teacher-
   led discussion paralleling Medieval middle class pilgrims to today's middle
   class people. Students usually develop a list that includes: teacher, nurse, wait-
   ress, teenager, custodian, soldier, cook, dishwasher, C.E.O, salesman, postal
   worker, etc.
2. After the list is generated, each group or individual will pick one modern day,
   middle-class pilgrim to write about. Students can choose to work alone or
   with a partner.
3. Distribute Writing Your Own Canterbury Tale rubric and assignment sheet.
   Each group or individual must create a 40 or 60 line tale in the style of
   Chaucer. Each line must contain roughly ten syllables, and lines must be
   rhyming couplets.

J.K. Dowdy and S. Kaplan, Teaching Drama in the Classroom, 75–76.

4. Students will have three days in class to work on creating their tale. This gives students time to collaborate with their partners and share with me and ask questions because rhyming metric verse takes time and several revisions.
5. After these three days, students will use the school computers to begin recording their tale. Students are shown a PowerPoint presentation on how to use Audacity. Audacity is a software program that allows students to record their voice and turn the recording into a MP3 and Podcast. Students will have the opportunity to play around with the program, listening to their voices and getting used to all the features.
6. The next day students will be given the chance to record their tales with head-mics. Students have the chance to record and re-record, edit and mix audio tracks to create a final copy.
7. On day six, students will learn how to search for free audio clips and save these effects to MP3 format so they can be imported into the program. Students will continue recording, adding in sound effects and music to make their tale character specific.
8. On the eighth day, student tales are due. Students will convert their tales into MP3 format and the teacher saves each tale on a USB drive. Then, the teacher will burn these tales on to a CD so we can listen to them in class.
9. Finally, students and teachers will gather together to listen to the student created tales. Students will need to fill out a critique of each student's tale. We will vote as a class on the best tale. That group or individual will win a free dinner, just like the winner in the original *The Canterbury Tales.*

Content Rubric

_____ Contains 10 syllables per line (20 pts)
_____ Maintains Chaucerian rhyme scheme (aa, bb, cc) (20 pts)
_____ 40 or 60 lines minimum (15 pts)
_____ Poem is either a prologue or tale of your character (10 pts)
_____ Recorded tale is easy to hear, well-annunciated (15 pts)
_____ Recording has at least 3 sound effects (10 pts)
_____ Recording has music (10 pts)

HEATHER ORIS

DRAMA ACTIVITY: PEER TEACHING
THROUGH PERFORMANCES

RATIONALE

Teaching drama through peer teaching is an activity that can be used with students of all ages. This peer teaching activity develops higher-level reading skills, writing skills, and public speaking skills. It also engages students and allows them to take ownership of their education. For this particular activity, the students deeply analyze *The Odyssey* in order to compose their own modernized version of the story through the creation of a script. Then, the students perform this modern tale for the class complete with scenery, music, and props. While this unit can be very challenging, students love *The Odyssey* after this unit because they find it engaging and collaborative.

STEPS

1. Students select their group members and the section of *The Odyssey* their group wishes to read.
2. Students read their section of *The Odyssey* independently and take notes along the way on characters and plot. They also plot the action of the story and answer the study questions given by the teacher.
3. Students meet in their groups and discuss their section of *The Odyssey* to try to make meaning together.
4. Students translate the story and create a script using more modern dialogue.
5. Students then add at least one creative piece to their performance. They may choose a song to capture the mood of the story, design artwork or scenery, or bring in three props to add to their performance.
6. Students choose roles and perform their section of *The Odyssey* as a way to teach the class Homer's classic.
7. The audience attempts to answer study questions on the section performed to see how much they learned from the performance and how thoroughly the group covered the story in their script.

EXTENSIONS

1. Prior to the start of this group activity, read one book from *The Odyssey* together and model the activity for the class using improvisation.

J.K. Dowdy and S. Kaplan, Teaching Drama in the Classroom, 77–78.

2. Provide opportunities for students to study their character prior to delivering their performance.
3. Have the students find epic conventions in their section and teach them to the class in a creative way (ex. Jeopardy).

MARY TOEPFER

BRING THE STORY TO LIFE: USING DRAMA WITH LITERATURE

"I have no idea what those characters are saying! I don't understand their language!" or "Why do we have to learn this stuff?" Such words were often what my high school students said when confronted with a Shakespearean play or a text written in another time period. Reading selections in high school British, American, or World Literature anthologies are sometimes difficult texts for students, or they present topics that students cannot possibly understand without putting themselves into the shoes of the characters involved. Hence, I tend to use improvisational dramatic episodes as a pre-reading strategy for challenging literature. This seems to help secondary students ahead of time to become familiar with the topic or characters about which they'll read in texts assigned for homework.

American Literature anthologies typically include an excerpt from Frederick Douglass's second autobiography *My Bondage and My Freedom* (usually the chapter entitled "A Change Came o'er the Spirit of my Dream" or Chapter XI), which focuses on the reality that slaves were not permitted the opportunity to read and write, something that students today probably take for granted; and British literature anthologies typically include Shakespeare's *Macbeth*, which highlights the consequences of excessive ambition, a message that often gets lost due to the rich, colorful language of the great Bard. As a result, I have developed pre-reading drama workshops for those two particular texts.

In the first workshop I present below, students step into the role of slaves or slave owners, bringing background knowledge to poetry about slavery as well as preparing for the topics they will encounter in the Frederick Douglass narrative about his life as a slave. Students learn through the second workshop about Shakespeare's timeless themes as they replicate the plot of *Macbeth* by presenting a modern version set in a high school.

The first workshop also highlights the value of using writing as a drama strategy. I use this, then, as a way of introducing my pre-service teachers to process drama in a college course specifically designed to teach literacy strategies across the content areas. I want them to see that it is important to build gradually their students' roles in a drama through the process of writing so that improvisation can come more naturally. Using the topic of slavery about which most students have some background knowledge, the pre-service teachers transact with poetry about slavery, assume a position (as either a slave or a slave owner), create an identity

J.K. Dowdy and S. Kaplan, Teaching Drama in the Classroom, 79–86.

for themselves, discuss in a journal their day as that person, and decide how they feel about a topic from that person's perspective, all before they engage in conversation about that topic with a partner from the opposing camp. The topic becomes the reason for the drama and inspires students to read the text for homework—the mission of a pre-reading activity, of course.

FREDERICK DOUGLASS DRAMA WORKSHOP: INTRODUCTION

Read aloud a good poem or two about slavery. Some suggestions: "The Slave Auction" by Frances E. W. Harper (in Hughes & Bontemps, 1970, p. 14); "I, Too, Sing America" by Langston Hughes (in Hughes & Bontemps, 1970, p. 182); "Southern Mansion" by Arna Bontemps (in Manley & O'Neill, 1997, pp. 105–106); "No Images" by Waring Cuney (in Bontemps, 1941, p. 28).

Have students circle words and phrases that appeal to the senses as you read the poems together. Make lists on the board. For example, students might highlight these words from "The Slave Auction": *stifled sobs, bitter cries, streaming eyes, bartered, hue, shrinking children, wept, lifeless clay, torn away, dull and heavy weight.* Such words help readers to understand the heaviness of slaves being sold at auction by feeling the event with their senses. Ask students to think about what it would be like to purchase a person to become their slave and, conversely, to think about what it would be like to be purchased to become someone else's slave.

WHAT TO DO

1. To begin the drama, have students determine what slave life was like and what the slave owners' lives were like, using background knowledge together with sensory images given in the poems discussed above. Students make lists of characteristics/adjectives at their seats.
2. Form students into two groups that face each other. One group becomes the slaves; the other group becomes those inside the mansion. (Anita Manley and Cecily O'Neill, 1997, highlight a similar strategy by having students read "Southern Mansion" and creating two tableaux from their transactions with the poem: one displaying the slaves' quarters and one displaying life in the mansion. They inspired my writing-in-role activity below.)
3. Have students write out who they are within their group. Ask them to answer: "What is your name? Where are you? What time of day is it? Who makes decisions for you? What went on in your world today?" Then, ask students to create a diary entry of their day as that person. Some examples of what students might create are as follows:

(From the perspective of a daughter in the mansion:)

Dear Diary,

This house is so big that sometimes I feel so small inside of it. There is the parlor, library, kitchen, garden. I feel as though I could disappear for hours somewhere and not be found. Anyway, I smell food cooking; it smells like the kitchen help is making us a delicious dinner. I have to have a sewing lesson soon, and I really don't want to go to it. I hate sewing. But I am a girl so I must do what I'm told, right? I am tired of that. I mean, I might as well be one of the slaves, and that is so wrong! Something must be done. No one should have to live like that. I'm doing my part, though. I have a secret: I have been teaching the stable boy how to read without my parents catching on. We have been meeting in the evenings behind the big willow tree for the past month, and he is really progressing. His name is Henry and he is so nice. He is my age, so I just use my own books to teach him. I don't understand why people make such a big deal about the colored folks being different from the whites. When I look at it and think about it, we really aren't different at all. Henry loves to read and learn, just as I do. He even loves apple pie, just as I do. But I am scared. If someone finds out, we could be in big trouble and he could get hurt. I don't want that to happen. Yet, I will not stop teaching him. I think that I want to be a teacher one day. I would like it a lot, but I want to teach *everyone*, not just those whom people think I should teach. Time to sew. Write soon.

Tara

(From the perspective of a teenage boy in the mansion:)

Dear Diary:

I woke up to humidity hitting me in my face and begging for some lemonade. Soon I will be forced to go to Europe as my father insists that is where a proper Southern gentleman is to get an education. He himself went to Harvard up North and studied law. I managed to get dressed and, in a matter of seconds, got my lemonade handed to me and began to sip it on the veranda, waiting for my schoolteacher to get ready for today's lesson. I began to daydream of Jeanie with the light brown hair. How can I leave her for the years it will take to get my education?

George Thomas, 1847

4. Using pair play, students now need to have a conversation with someone from the opposite camp, explaining their feelings about a situation highlighted in their diary entries. First, though, make a list together on the board of the reasons that two folks from different camps would talk to each other. Some examples include the following:

 a) Owner is giving slave a list of tasks to do.
 b) Boy slave and girl owner are having a secret affair or girl slave and male owner are having an affair.
 c) Owner is teaching slave how to do something.
 d) Slave is asking owner for some privilege.
 e) Slave is accepting a gift from owner or vice versa.
 f) Slave and owner are friends and are hanging out.

SAMPLE DISCUSSION

(Between Myra Johnson, a slave, and Emma, the slave owner's daughter:)

Myra: You wanna try a bite of my gumbo, Miss Emma?
Emma: Sure! I love your gumbo! (*lifts spoon to her nose and smells*) Mmmmm. Smells fabulous! (*tastes it*) Tastes perfect!
Myra: Thanks, sugar. You are my best critic. Your mama has a whole lotta folks comin' and I want to make sure they're well fed.
Emma: I know. I wish I could just stay here in the kitchen with you, Myra. You are much more fun to be around than those stuffy ladies.
Myra: It's not proper, miss, for the ladies of the house to be fraternizin' with the help, you know. But I do enjoy your company, and your good taste in gumbo. Besides, you will look lovely in that beautiful dress your mother wants you to wear! I just love to look at all the gorgeous dresses.
Emma: Don't you have pretty dresses, Myra?
Myra: No, sweetie, but I wish! I just have the clothes on my back. Of course, I'm thankful all the same.
Emma: When I get older, Myra, I'll be sure to get you a pretty dress all your own!

End of scene

 5. At this point, students have established an identity as well as distinct feelings about slaves, making it easier for them to form an opinion from that perspective about the following question: What if I told you that you were not allowed to learn how to read and write (if you were a slave) or that you were not allowed to teach slaves to read and write (if you were a slave owner)? How would you feel? What's your opinion on the topic? Write out a list of why a slave should/should not be able to read and write (those playing the role of slaves might now say that they are among those who can't write, so encourage them to dictate their thoughts to someone else who can). Write out a list of why slave owners should/should not teach slaves to read and write. What are the benefits and drawbacks of each? Teachers may provide a discussion web for this part for students to use.
 6. Have students go back to their pair play group, now that they have had a chance to think this through. Ask them: What would you say to each other about this specific issue of reading and writing?

After students complete the activities above, introduce Frederick Douglass by reading a selection from *A Picture Book of Frederick Douglass* by David A. Adler, particularly the two pages which talk about how his master's wife taught him how to read and then suddenly stopped teaching him. Explain to students that for homework they will be reading more about Frederick Douglass in the textbook excerpt from *My Bondage and My Freedom.*

MACBETH DRAMA WORKSHOP

WHAT TO DO

Before students read the play, the teacher walks into the classroom in the role of the principal of William Shakespeare Memorial High School. The principal explains that she has just been given an anonymous letter from a concerned student about some unfairness happening to Duncan King, a popular senior student. The principal wants to get to the bottom of the situation by attending a class containing seniors who know all the players involved. The letter explains that Lisa Marie Bloodthirsty seems to be excessively ambitious and, with the help of her boyfriend Matt Glamis, attempts to do something awful to Duncan. He apparently has something that they want. One way to introduce the tension to the students is for the principal to show them the letter written by the concerned student (below) in which the characters' names and personalities are described. The concerned student also overheard enough of the conversation between Matt and Lisa Marie that he/she provides that information in the letter the principal reads aloud.

Out of role, the teacher should break students into groups of three and have them write their account of what they heard happened, using the teacher-selected lines from Shakespeare's *Macbeth* (Act I) in addition to lines of their own. Upon reading aloud the teacher-selected lines and asking students to discuss what is implied about the speaker of each line before letting them create their scenes, the teacher should allow roughly 20 minutes for them to prepare a scene. Each group presents its scenes by acting them out. Then, the teacher should close the episode by becoming the principal again, taking the information the students provide, and running off to make phone calls.

Principal: Hello students. I'm standing before you today because something awful has happened here at William Shakespeare Memorial High School. Someone in this school has been treated unfairly and I demand to know exactly how! All I know is what's been provided to me in this anonymous letter:

Dear Principal Wilma Quiverblade,

I think you should know that two of your students are up to no good. Senior Duncan King seems to have something that these students have been wanting, and they went too far this time to get it. I mean, sure, who wouldn't want what Duncan King has? He's class president, captain of the football team, and brilliant and wealthy to boot. He drives his little red sports car around and keeps up with the latest fashion trends. Better than all of that, though, is the fact that his popularity hasn't gone to his head. He's super nice to everyone and certainly didn't provoke his classmates' quest.

I suggest you question Matt Glamis and his girlfriend, Lisa Marie Blood-thirsty, if you want to know more about this situation. Lisa Marie has always been so driven to be popular that she'll stop at nothing. Her latest kick is to be number one in every activity so that she can get into the best college. I'm sure you noticed that she's gotten all A's this semester and is involved in more clubs and activities than anybody else in the school. Matt needs to appease her driven spirit by jumping on board her ship to Popularville or else she'll dump him. I'm certain that Matt doesn't care about being popular, but I guess opposites attract. Although he and Duncan have been friends for years, Matt allowed Lisa Marie to talk him into her malicious plan.

By the way, I was able to overhear some of what was said when this went down. Unfortunately, all that I can provide to you are the words below. I hope they will help you to piece together what happened so that such a travesty will not be repeated at our school.

Sincerely,

A CONCERNED STUDENT

I dare do all that may become a man ...

Look like th' innocent flower ...

Speak, if you can ...

We will proceed no further in this business.

My dull brain was wrought with things forgotten.

Let not light see my black and deep desires.

Thou'rt mad to say it!

Principal: Well, as you can imagine, I haven't been able to find any of them, even Duncan. I have a call in to their parents but wanted to come directly to you who know all of them best to get some answers. Can you please tell me what you know?

Sample Scene

Lisa Marie: Hi, Miss Secretary. We'd like to decorate Duncan King's locker for the upcoming football game to wish him well! Could you get a janitor to let us into it so we can put a treat bag inside? (*winks at Matt*)

Sally Secretary: Sure! (*on loud speaker*) Custodian Smith, please come to the office. Thank you.

(*pause*)

Custodian Smith: Here I am! What can I do for you, Sally?

Sally Secretary: Well, these kids here would like to decorate Duncan's locker for the game. Could you let them into it, please? "Speak, if you can . . ."

Custodian Smith: Sure thing. Follow me, kids. (*walks out; leads Lisa Marie and Matt down the hallway to Duncan's locker and then unlocks it for them.*)

Custodian Smith: Oh, "My dull brain was wrought with things forgotten." I forgot that I was supposed to be setting up the tables in the library for the luncheon today. Gotta run, kids. Have fun!

Lisa Marie (*smiling brightly*): Thanks so much! We really appreciate it!

(*Custodian Smith leaves quickly; Lisa Marie stops smiling as soon as he's out of sight.*)

Lisa Marie: Okay, Matt, let's get that bag of drugs inside, but "Look like th' innocent flower . . . ."

Matt: "I dare do all that may become a man. . . .

(*Sounds as though someone is coming, so Matt closes the locker door.*)

Matt: "We will proceed no further in this business."

Lisa Marie: What? "Thou'rt mad to say it!" We've come this far! Let's just hurry up. We have to make this locker look decorated. No one will question a thing if the locker looks nice.

Matt: Okay. "Let not light see my black and deep desires." I really do want to be the team captain, so if this gets Duncan out of the way, then so be it.

(*The two finish decorating the locker*)

Lisa Marie: Okay, let's call the cops and tell them that they need to get the dogs in the school to sniff the lockers today. Duncan won't know what hit him!

(*Matt nods. They leave quickly.*)

End of scene

This pre-reading activity familiarizes students with the basic premise of the play as well as the key theme of excessive ambition. It also highlights the manipulative qualities of Lady Macbeth and introduces students to the language of Shakespeare that they will encounter in their reading of Act I for homework.

Using drama as a pre-reading activity, in general, places students into the lives of the characters about whom they will read, either directly or indirectly. I have found that there really is no better way to ensure that students fully understand the decisions the characters make or the words they say than to have students step into their shoes and *become* them. The words become less daunting and the characters' actions become more logical, especially since these characters are from a distant time period for students; but the best reason to use improvisation is really for the fun of it!

REFERENCES

Adler, D. A. (1993). *A picture book of Frederick Douglass*. (S. Byrd, Illus.). New York: Holiday House.

Bontemps, A. (ed.) (1941). *GoldenSslippers: An anthology of Negro poetry for young readers*. New York: Harper & Row.

Hughes, L. & Bontemps, A. (eds.) (1970). *The poetry of the Negro, 1746–1970*. Garden City: Doubleday.

Manley, A. & O'Neill, C. (1997). *Dreamseekers: Creative approaches to the African American heritage*. Portsmouth, NH: Heinemann.

TERI POULOS

A WALK IN THE PARK

RATIONALE

In the course of reading a novel, it became clear that my students were struggling to keep track of the many characters, not to mention the action and meaning in the plot. While this particular incident occurred in a class of struggling readers, true involvement and understanding of the characters of a novel can be a problem for students of any level. Comprehension, class discussion and written responses to the literature all suffer when readers grapple with the basics of the text.

The options for review are many; however, in order to engage my students in the process, to allow them to collaborate with others and combine their bits of knowledge, and to break up the routine of reading and discussion, I devised this workshop. Additional benefits to this method of formative assessment were that it provided the information the students and I needed, it was immediate, and it did not create more paperwork.

WHAT TO DO

1. Select a place (real or imaginary) from the novel where the characters might happen upon one another and interact.
2. Prepare a list or slips of paper with character names.
3. Create a space in the room that adequately mimics the space in the novel. Have the students sit in an audience space surrounding the dramatic space.
4. Assign characters to students. If there are more students than characters, they can work in groups. Give students a few minutes to talk about and jot down notes about the involvement of the character in the plot, the character's personality, interests, motivations.
5. Explain the dramatic situation to the students. Tell them that they will be called to the dramatic space in pairs, and for a few minutes they will improvise an interaction between the two characters. While the two selected "actors" should initiate the interaction, the audience can also call out suggestions for the interaction.
6. Remind students that posture and body language contribute to communication and should be employed in the drama.
7. If necessary, begin by demonstrating the action by taking on a character yourself and interacting with a volunteer.
8. Call the first pair. You may orchestrate the pairings or draw names randomly.

J.K. Dowdy and S. Kaplan, Teaching Drama in the Classroom, 87–88.
© 2011. *Sense Publishers. All rights reserved.*

9. As the pair enters the dramatic space, prompt them as needed to take on the personality of the characters. Encourage the audience to help the actors interact by making suggestions.

10. Allow the interaction to continue as long as it is productive. If the students (audience and actors) fail to bring up an important aspect of the character's personality or past, prompt them using questions.

11. When the drama is complete, have the actors take leave of one another appropriately and return to the audience. Call the next couple.

SAMPLE

Using *Witness* by Karen Hesse (2001).

Dramatic space: A path along the river in the town. A "bench" along that path where townspeople can sit to contemplate the river or chat with a friend.

Preparations: Lay a long piece of paper on the floor as "the path." Place a couple of chairs side by side to represent the bench.

Leonora and Merlin are called to the dramatic space.

Leonora walks slowly down the path to the bench and sits to watch the river. Merlin enters path. When he comes near, Leonora tenses up and perches on the edge of the bench nervously. Merlin sits on the other side of the bench as far from her as possible. A few minutes of silence.

Merlin, starting quietly, nervously: I saw you the other day.

Leonora, also quietly, first looking up to see if he is indeed talking to her: Me? What do you mean?

Merlin: When you saved the Jew kid.

Leonora: By the railroad tracks? You were there?

Merlin: Yeah. I saw you running.

Leonora: Esther was about to be hit by the train. I was lucky to get there.

Merlin: You ran like a deer. I couldn't believe you got there in time.

Leonora: I just did what had to be done. Anyone would have done the same. She's only six, and it was like she wanted to get hit. You would have done it if you could.

Merlin: No. Not me.

Leonora: Hmm. (Pause. Audience prompt: What about school?) You going to come back to school?

Merlin: Nah. I got a job. I'm working for Mr. Alexander at the paper. It's a good job.

Leonora: I guess. (Long silence. Eventually they leave without another word.)

BRANDY MCFEE

CHARACTER INTERVIEWS

The Character Interview is a drama activity that can be used with students of all ages and in almost any class, with some modifications. The activity can be used as a during-reading or an after-reading activity. It encourages higher-order thinking and addresses many Reading Applications: Literary Text and Reading Process benchmarks, such as asking/answering questions, analyzing character, identifying viewpoints, etc. The activity has students ask questions to characters from a book and then respond to the questions in the voice of one of the characters. The only materials needed are the text being used in class and pieces of paper on which to write character names. This activity works well for both the teacher and the students because the students get to have fun role-playing characters while reviewing and examining a piece of text, and the teacher can see how well the students understand the characters and the text.

PROCEDURES

1. It is best to prepare ahead of time a list of the main characters from the book and then put them on slips of paper to have students draw from. This makes sure everyone is not doing the same character and no can argue about who gets which character.
2. Students draw a character's name from the prepared slips in step one.
3. Students create 5 questions they would want to ask that particular character (the teacher may assign more or fewer questions depending on the students).

    a) The questions should *not* be yes/no type questions.
    b) The teacher may want to give some examples for the students to help them along: How did you feel when ...? What would happen if ...? Why did you ...? When did you ...?
    c) Questions don't have to be about things that happen in the book. For instance, students may have questions about what happened to the character after the book ended or before it began.

4. The teacher gives students about five minutes or so to write the questions.
5. Students then pair up with another student, but *not* someone with the same character.

J.K. Dowdy and S. Kaplan, Teaching Drama in the Classroom, 89–90.

6. Students then take turns asking their partners their questions, but the responder *must* answer the question *as if they are that character*!

   *Ex: Student A draws Bella and Student B draws Edward from *Twilight*.

   1. Student A writes 5 questions for Bella and Student B writes 5 questions for Edward.
   2. Student A asks Student B the Bella questions and Student B must answer them as if he or she is Bella.
   3. Then roles reverse and Student B asks Student A the Edward questions and Student A must answer them as if he or she is Edward.
7. The teacher should walk around the room listening to each group's questions/answers to make sure they are on task and staying true to the character.
8. After each group seems finished, the teacher asks for volunteers to share with the class.

EXTENSIONS/VARIATIONS

1. Students may hold a longer conversation with each other as their characters, using the questions as a starting point.
2. Many writing activities can come from this exercise, such as writing journal entries from the character's viewpoint.
3. Outside of the language arts room, students can do this same activity with important figures from other content areas (presidents, explorers, artists, scientists, animals, etc.).
4. For younger students the teacher may have questions prepared ahead of time or create questions together with students.

CHARACTER LIST

The Skin I'm In by Sharon Flake

* Maleeka Madison
* Miss Saunders
* Charlese (Char)
* John-John McIntrye
* Caleb
* Mrs. Madison

Number the Stars by Lois Lowry

* Annemarie Johansen
* Mrs. Johansen
* Peter Nielsen
* Henrik
* Ellen Rosen
* Mr. Johansen

JESSICA CERVENAK

TO KILL A MOCKINGBIRD: DRAMA LESSON

RATIONALE

This lesson was created to help students connect to the text *To Kill a Mockingbird* through dramatizing the trial, which takes place in chapter 17 of the novel. The objectives of the lesson were to enable students to understand the novel by acting out the scene as a class and to use prior knowledge of the characters to effectively portray each one's emotions during the trial. The lesson provides the opportunity for kinesthetic learners to actually stand up and act out the scene while at the same time meeting the needs of auditory learners who are able to hear the interaction between the characters.

WHAT TO DO

1. The students read chapter 17 on their own for homework.
2. The class discusses the various characters who are present in the court scene and create a list of characteristics that have been developed both directly and indirectly by the author for each character. After the discussion is complete, the teacher facilitates a discussion about the emotions of each character during the trial.
3. The teacher assigns parts and have the students read assigned parts for homework. There are not enough parts for each student in class, so the students who do have parts are graded on their ability to bring the character to life, while the rest of the class is responsible for evaluating and giving constructive criticism to the student actors.
4. During the next class meeting, the teacher has the students read through the script as a class. An additional requirement may be for the students to dress as if they are the character they are portraying. The classroom should be set up as a courtroom and props are strongly encouraged to help set up the atmosphere.
5. After the scene is acted out, all the students should write a reflection based on what they learned from the scene. Students who played the part of a character should discuss how they think their character felt in this scene as well as what they learned from the experience. Students who were a part of the audience should pick a character and discuss what they think that character was feeling throughout the scene as well as what they learned about the book as a result of this scene.

J.K. Dowdy and S. Kaplan, Teaching Drama in the Classroom, 91–108.

JESSICA CERVENAK

SCRIPT

MR. GILMER: ... in your own words, Mr. Tate.

MR. TATE: Well (touching glasses and speaking to his knees), I was called—

MR. GILMER: Could you say it to the jury, Mr. Tate? Thank you. Who called you?

MR. TATE: I was fetched by Bob—by Mr. Bob Ewell yonder, one night?

MR. GILMER: What night, Sir?

MR. TATE: It was the night of November twenty-first. I was just leaving my office to go home when B—Mr. Ewell came in, very excited he was, and said get out to his house quick, some black man raped his girl.

MR. GILMER: Did you go?

MR. TATE: Certainly. Got in the car and went out as fast as I could.

MR. GILMER: And what did you find?

MR. TATE: Found her lying on the floor in the middle of the front room, one on the right as you go in. She was pretty well beat up, but I heaved her to her feet and she washed her face in a bucket in the corner and said she was all right. I asked her who hurt her and she said it was Tom Robinson—Asked her if he beat her like that, she said yes he had. Asked her if he took advantage of her and she said yes he did. So, I went down to Robinson's house and brought him back. She identified him as the one, so I took him in. That's all there was to it.

MR. GILMER: Thank you.

JUDGE TAYLOR: Any questions, Atticus?

ATTICUS: Yes. Did you call a doctor, Sheriff? Did anybody call a doctor?

MR. TATE: No, Sir.

ATTICUS: Didn't call a doctor?

MR. TATE: No, Sir.

ATTICUS: Why not?

MR. TATE: Well, I can tell you why I didn't. It wasn't necessary, Mr. Finch. She was mighty banged up. Something sho' happened, it was obvious.

ATTICUS: But you didn't call a doctor? While you were there did anyone send for one, fetch one, carry her to one?

MR. TATE: No, Sir.

JUDGE TAYLOR: He's answered the question three times, Atticus. He didn't call a doctor. ATTICUS: I just wanted to make sure, Judge. Sheriff, you say she was mighty banged up. In what way?

MR. TATE: Well—

ATTICUS: Just describe her injuries, Heck.

MR. TATE: Well, she was beaten around the head. There was already bruises comin' on her arms, and it happened about thirty minutes before—

ATTICUS: How do you know?

MR. TATE: Sorry, that's what they said. Anyway, she was pretty bruised up when I got there, and she had a black eye comin'.

ATTICUS: Which eye?

MR. TATE (softly): Let's see.

ATTICUS: Can't you remember?

MR. TATE (pointing to an invisible person five inches in form of him): Her left.

ATTICUS: Wait a minute, Sheriff. Was it her left facing you or her left looking the same way you were?

MR. TATE: Oh yes, that'd make it her right. It was her right eye, Mr. Finch. I remember now, she was bunged up on that side of her face ...

ATTICUS: Sheriff, please repeat what you said.

MR. TATE: It was her right eye.

ATTICUS: No (walking over to the court reporter).

COURT REPORTER (reading from the pad): "Mr. Finch. I remember now she was bunged up on that side of the face."

ATTICUS: Which side again, Heck?

MR. TATE: The right side, Mr. Finch, but she had more bruises–you wanta hear about 'em? ATTICUS: Yes, what were her other injuries?

MR. TATE: Her arms were bruised, and she showed me her neck. There were definite finger marks on her gulle—

ATTICUS: All around her throat? At the back of her neck?

MR. TATE: I'd say they were all around, Mr. Finch.

ATTICUS: You would?

MR. TATE: Yes, Sir, she had a small throat, anybody could'a reached around it with—

ATTICUS: Just answer the question yes or no, please, Sheriff. (Atticus sits down and nods to the circuit solicitor.)

CLERK: Robert E. Lee Ewell. (Bob goes to the chair and is sworn in.)

BOB EWELL: —so help me God.

MR. GILMER: Mr. Robert Ewell?

BOB EWELL: That's m'name, cap'n.

MR. GILMER: Are you the father of Mayella Ewell?

BOB EWELL: Well, if I ain't I can't do nothing about it now, her ma's dead.
JUDGE TAYLOR: Are you the father of Mayella Ewell?

BOB EWELL: Yes, Sir.

JUDGE TAYLOR: This the first time you've been in court? I don't recall ever seeing you here. (Witness Bob nods head.) Well, let's get something straight. There will be no more audibly obscene speculations on any subject from anybody in this courtroom as long as I'm sitting here. Do you understand? All right, Mr. Gilmer.

MR. GILMER: Thank you, sir. Mr. Ewell, would you tell us in your own words what happened on the evening of November twenty-first, please?

BOB EWELL: Well, the night of November twenty-one I was comin' in from the woods with a load o'kindlin' and just as I got to the fence I heard Mayella screamin' like a stuck hog inside the house—

MR. GILMER: What time was it, Mr. Ewell?

BOB EWELL: Just 'fore sundown. Well, I was sayin' Mayella was screamin' fit to beat Jesus—

MR. GILMER: Yes? She was screaming?

BOB EWELL: Well, Mayella was raisin' this holy racket so I dropped m'load and run as fast as I could but I run into th' fence, but when I got distangled I run up to th' window and I seen— (stands up and points his finger at Tom Robinson) I seen that black man yonder ruttin' on my Mayella!

JUDGE TAYLOR (banging his gavel): There has been a request, that this court-room be cleared of spectators, or at least of women and children, a request that will be denied for the time being. People generally see what they look for, and hear what they listen for, and they have the right to subject their children to it, but you won't leave it until the whole boiling of you come before me on contempt charges. Mr. Ewell, you will keep your testimony within the confines of Christian English usage, if that is possible. Proceed, Mr. Gilmer.

MR. GILMER: You say you were at the window?

BOB EWELL: Yes, sir.

MR. GILMER: How far is it from the ground?

BOB EWELL: 'Bout three foot.

MR. GILMAR: Did you have a clear view of the room?

BOB EWELL: Yes, sir.

MR. GILMAR: How did the room look?

BOB EWELL: Well, it was all slung about, like there was a fight.

MR. GI.LMAR: What did you do when you saw the defendant?

BOB EWELL: Well, I run around the house to get in, but he run out the front door just ahead of me. I sawed who he was, all right. I was too distracted about Mayella to run after 'im. I run in the house and she was lyin' on the floor squallin'—

MR. GILMAR: Then what did you do?

BOB EWELL: Why, I run for Tate quick as I could. I knowed who it was, all right, lived down yonder in that nigger-nest, passed the house every day, Jedge, I've asked this county for fifteen years to clean out that nest down yonder, they're dangerous to live around 'sides devaluin' my property—

MR. GILMAR: Thank you, Mr. Ewell.

ATTICUS: Just a minute, sir. Could I ask you a question or two? Mr. Ewell, folks were doing a lot of running that night. Let's see, you say you ran to the house, you ran to the window, you ran inside, you ran to Mayella, you ran for Mr. Tate. Did you, during all this running, run for a doctor?

BOB EWELL: Wadn't no need to. I seen what happened.

ATTICUS: But there's one thing I don't understand. Weren't you concerned with Mayella's condition?

BOB EWELL: I most positively was, I seen who done it.

ATTICUS: No, I mean her physical condition. Did you not think the nature of her injuries warranted immediate medical attention?

BOB EWELL: What?

ATTICUS: Didn't you think she should have had a doctor, immediately?

BOB EWELL: That all?

ATTICUS: Not quite. Mr. Ewell, you heard the sheriff's testimony, didn't you?

BOB EWELL: How's that?

ATTICUS: You were in the courtroom when Mr. Heck Tate was on the stand, weren't you? You heard everything he said, didn't you?

BOB EWELL: Yes.

ATTICUS: Do you agree with his description of Mayella's injuries?

BOB EWELL: How's that?

ATTICUS: Mr. Tate testifies that her right eye was blackened, that she was beaten around the—

BOB EWELL: Oh yeah, I hold with everything Tate said.

ATTICUS: You do? I just want to make sure. (Atticus has the reporter read the testimony again.)

COURT REPORTER: Which eye her left oh yes tha'd make it her right it was her right eye Mr. Finch I remember now she was bunged. Up on that side of the face Sheriff please repeat what you said it was her right eye I said—

ATTICUS: Thank you, Bert. You heard it again, Mr. Ewell. Do you have anything to add to it? Do you agree with the sheriff?

BOB EWELL: I holds with Tate. Her eye was blacked and she was might beat up. ATTICUS: Mr. Ewell, can you read and write?

MR. GILMER: Objection. Can't see what witness's literacy has to do with the case, irrelevant' n' immaterial.

ATTICUS: Judge, if you'll allow the question, plus another one, you'll soon see.

JUDGE TAYLOR: All right, let's see. But make sure we see, Atticus. Overruled.

ATTICUS: I'll repeat the question. Can you read and write.

BOB EWELL: I most positively can.

ATTICUS: Will you write your name and show us?

BOB EWELL: I most positively will. How do you think I sign my relief checks?

ATTICUS: Would you write your name for us? Clearly now, so the jury can see you do it.

BOB EWELL: What's so interesting?

JUDGE TAYLOR: You're left-handed, Mr. Ewell.

MR. GILMER: About your writing with you left hand, are you ambidextrous, Mr. Ewell?

BOB EWELL: I most positively am not, I can use one hand good as the other. One hand good as the other. (Bob steps down from the witness stand.)

CLERK: Mayella Violet Ewell! (Mayella is sworn in.)

MR. GILMER: Where were you at dusk on the evening of November twenty-first?

MAYELLA: On the porch.

MR. GILMER: What porch?

MAYELLA: Ain't but one, the front porch.

JUDGE TAYLOR: Just tell us what happened. You can do that, can't you?

MAYELLA (bursts into tears): —

JUDGE TAYLOR: That's enough now. Don't be 'fraid of anybody here, as long as you tell the truth. All this is strange to you, I know, but you've nothing to be ashamed of and nothing to fear. What are you scared of? (Mayella says something under her breath.) What was that?

MAYELLA: Him!!! (sobs, pointing at Atticus)

JUDGE TAYLOR: Mr. Finch?

MAYELLA: Don't want him doin' me like he done Papa, tryin' to make him out lefthanded . . .

JUDGE TAYLOR: How old are you?

MAYELLA: Nineteen and a half.

JUDGE TALOR: Mr. Finch has no idea of scaring you, and if he did, I'm here to stop him. That's one thing I'm sitting up here for. Now, you're a big girl, so you just sit up straight and tell the—tell us what happened to you. You can do that, can't you?

MAYELLA: Well, sir, I was on the porch and—and he came along and, you see, there was this old chiffarobe in the yard Papa'd brought in to chop up for kindlin'—Papa told me to do it while he was off in the woods but I wadn't feelin' strong enough then, so he came by—

MR. GILMAR: Who is he?

MAYELLA: (points to Tom Robinson)

MR. GILMAR: I'll have to ask you to be more specific, please. The reporter can't put down gestures very well.

MAYELLA: That'n younder. Robinson.

MR. GILMAR: Then what happened?

MAYELLA: I said come here and bust up this chiffarobe for me, I gotta nickel for you. He coulda done it easy enough, he could. So he come in the yard an' I went in the house to get him the nickel and I turned around and 'fore I knew it he was on me. Just run up behind me, he did. He got me round the neck, cussin' me an' sayin' dirt—I fought an' hollered, but he had me round the neck. He hit me agin an' agin—(long pause waiting for Mr. Gilmar to ask another question, but he does not). He chunked me on the floor an' choked me an' took advantage of me.

MR. GILMAR: Did you scream? Did you scream and fight back?

MAYELLA: Reckon I did, hollered for all I was worth, kicked and hollered loud as I could.

MR. GILMAR: Then what happened?

MAYELLA: I don't remember too good, but next thing I knew Papa was in the room an' standing over me hollerin' who done it, who done it? Then I sorta fainted an' the next thing I knew Mr. Tate was pullin' me up offa the floor and leadin' me to the water bucket.

MR. GILMAR: You say you fought him off as hard as you could? Fought him tooth and nail?

MAYELLA: I positively did.

MR. GILMAR: You are positive that he took full advantage of you?

MAYELLA: He done what he was after.

MR. GILMAR (wiping his forehead): That's all for the time being, but you stay there. I expect big bad Mr. Finch has some questions to ask you.

JUDGE TAYLOR: State will not prejudice the witness against counsel for the defense. At least not at this time.

ATTICUS: Miss Mayella. I won't try to scare you for a while, not yet. Let's just get acquainted. How old are you?

MAYELLA: Said I was nineteen, said it to the judge yonder.

ATTICUS: So you did, so you did, ma'am. You'll have to bear with me, Miss Mayella, I'm getting along and can't remember as well as I used to. I might ask you things you've already said before, but you'll give me an answer, won't you? Good.

MAYELLA: Won't answer a word you say long as you keep on mockin' me.

ATTICUS: Ma'am?

MAYELLA: Long's you keep on makin' fun o' me.

JUDGE TAYLOR: Mr. Finch is not making fun of you. What's the matter with you?

ATTICUS: Long's he keeps on callin' me ma'am an' sayin' Miss Mayella. I don't hafta take his sass, I ain't called upon to take it.

JUDGE TAYLOR: That's just Mr. Finch's way. We've done business in this court for years and years, and Mr. Finch is always courteous to everybody. He's not trying to mock you, he's trying to be polite. That's just his way. Atticus, let's get on with these proceedings, and let the record show that the witness has not been sassed, her views to the contrary.

ATTICUS: You say you're nineteen. How many sisters and brothers have you?

MAYELLA: Seb'n.

ATTICUS: You the eldest? The oldest?

MAYELLA: Yes.

ATTICUS: How long has your mother been dead?

MAYELLA: Don't know—long time.

ATTICUS: Did you ever go to school?

MAYELLA: Read an' write good as Pap yonder.

ATTICUS: How long did you go to school?

MAYELLA: Two year—three year—dunno.

ATTICUS: Miss Mayella, a nineteen-year-old girl like you must have friends. Who are your friends?

MAYELLA: Friends?

ATTICUS: Yes, don't you know anyone near your age, or older, or younger? Boys and girls? Just ordinary friends?

MAYELLA: You makin' fun o' me agin, Mr. Finch?

ATTICUS: Do you love your father, Miss Mayella?

MAYELLA: Love him, whatcha mean?

ATTICUS: I mean, is he good to you, is he easy to get along with?

MAYELLA: He does tolable, 'cept when—

ATTICUS: Except when?

MAYELLA: Except when nothing. I said he does tolable.

ATTICUS: Except when he's drinking? (Mayella nods.) Does he go after you?

MAYELLA: How you mean?

ATTICUS: When he?s?riled, has he ever beaten you?

JUDGE TAYLOR: Answer the question, Miss Mayella.

MAYELLA: My paw's never touched a hair o' my head in my life, he never touched me.

ATTICUS: We've had a good visit, Miss Mayella, and now I guess we'd better get to the case. You say you asked Tom Robinson to come chop up a—what was it?

MAYELLA: A chiffarobe, a old dresser full of drawers on one side.

ATTICUS: Was Tom Robinson well known to you?

MAYELLA: Whaddya mean?

ATTICUS: I mean did you know who he was, where he lived?

MAYELLA: I knowed who he was, he passed the house every day.

ATTICUS: Was this the first time you asked him to come inside the fence? (long pause, Atticus looks out the window. Mayella jumps at the question.) Was—?

MAYELLA: Yes, it was.

ATTICUS: Didn't you ever ask him to come inside the fence before?

MAYELLA: I did not, I certainly did not.

ATTICUS: One did not's enough. You never asked him to do odd jobs for you before?

MAYELLA: I mighta. There was several black people around.

ATTICUS: Can you remember any other occasions.

MAYELLA: No.

ATTICUS: All right, now to what happened. You said Tom Robinson was behind you in the room when you turned around, that right?

MAYELLA: Yes.

ATTICUS: You said he got you around the neck cussing and saying dirt—is that right?

MAYELLA: It's right.

ATTICUS: You say, "he caught me and choked me and took advantage of me"—is that right?

MAYELLA: That's what I said.

ATTICUS: Do you remember him beating you about the face? (pause; Mayella glances at Mr. Gilmar.) It's an easy question, Miss Mayella, so I'll try again. Do you remember him beating you about the face? (more sternly) Do you remember him beating you about the face?

MAYELLA: No, I don't recollect if he hit me. I mean yes I do, he hit me.

ATTICUS: Was your last sentence you answer?

MAYELLA: Huh? Yes, he hit—I just don't remember, I just don't remember … it all happened so quick.

JUDGE TAYLOR: Don't you cry, young woman—

ATTICUS: Let her cry if she wants to, Judge. We've got all the time in the world.

MAYELLA: I'll answer any question you got—get me up here an' mock me, will you? I'll answer any question you got—

ATTICUS: That's fine. There're only a few more. Miss Mayella, not to be tedious, you've testified that the defendant hit you, grabbed you around the neck, choked you, and took advantage of you. I want you to be sure you have the right man. Will you identify the man who raped you?

MAYELLA: I will, that's him right yonder.

ATTICUS: Tom, stand up. Let Miss Mayella have a good long look at you. Is this the man, Miss Mayella? (Tom stands up and everyone looks at him.) Is this the man who raped you?

MAYELLA: It most certainly is.

ATTICUS: How?

MAYELLA: I don't know how he done it, but he done it. I said it all happened so fast I—

ATTICUS: No, let's consider this calmly?

MR. GILMAR: Atticus is browbeating the witness.

JUDGE TAYLOR (laughing): Oh, sit down, Horace, he's doing nothing of the sort. If anything, the witness's brow-beating Atticus.

ATTICUS: Now, Miss Mayella, you've testified that the defendant choked and beat you—you didn't say that he sneaked up behind you and knocked you cold, but you turned around and there he was—(knocks on table with knuckles emphasizing the words) do you wish to reconsider any of your testimony?

MAYELLA: You want me to say something that didn't happen?

ATTICUS: No, ma'am, I want you to say something that did happen. Tell us once more, please, what happened?

MAYELLA: I told ya what happened.

ATTICUS: You testified that you turned around and there he was. He choked you then?

MAYELLA: Yes.

ATTICUS: Then he released your throat and hit you?

MAYELLA: I said he did.

ATTICUS: He blacked your left eye with his right fist?

MAYELLA: I ducked and it—it glanced, that's what it did. I ducked and it glanced off.

ATTICUS: You're becoming suddenly clear on this point. Awhile ago you couldn't remember too well, could you?

MAYELLA: I said he hit me.

ATTICUS: All right. He choked you, he hit you, then he raped you, that right?

MAYELLA: It most certainly is.

ATTICUS: You're a strong girl, what were you doing all the time, just standing there?

MAYELLA: I told ya, I hollered an' kicked an' fought—

(Atticus starts to rain questions on Mayella.)

JUDGE TALOR: One question at a time, Atticus. Give the witness a chance to answer.

ATTICUS: All right, why didn't you run?

MAYELLA: I tried.

ATTICUS: Tried to? What kept you from it?

MAYELLA: I—he slung me down. That's what he did, he slung me down an' got on top of me.

ATTICUS: You were screaming this whole time?

MAYELLA: I certainly was.

ATTICUS: Then why didn't the other children hear you? Where were they? At the dump? Where were they?

(no answer)

Why didn't your screams make them come running? The dump's closer than the woods, isn't it?

(no answer)

Or did you not scream until you saw your father in the window? You didn't think to scream until then, did you?

(no answer)

Did you scream first at your father instead of at Tom Robinson? Was that it?

(no answer)

Who beat you up? Tom Robinson or your father?

(no answer)

What did your father see in the window, the crime of rape or the best defense to it? Why don't you tell the truth, child, didn't Bob Ewell beat you up? (Atticus sits down and wipes his glasses.)

MAYELLA: I got somethin' to say.

ATTICUS: Do you want to tell us what happened?

MAYELLA: I got somethin' to say an' then I ain't gonna say no more. That black man yonder took advantage of me an' if you fine fancy gentlemen don't wanta do nothin' about it, then you're all yellow stinkin' cowards, stinkin' cowards, the lot of you. Your fancy airs don't come to nothin'—your ma'amin' and Miss Mayellerin' don't come to nothin', Mr. Finch?

MR. GILMER: The state rests its case.

JUDGE TAYLOR: It's time we all did. We'll take ten minutes.

(Atticus and Mr. Gilmer meet in front of the bench and whisper.)

(Tom walks up to swear in, puts his right hand in the air and the left one on the Bible. His useless hand falls off the Bible.)

JUDGE TAYLOR: That'll do, Tom

ATTICUS: Have you ever been in trouble with the law before?

TOM ROBINSON: Yes, I once received thirty days for disorderly conduct.

ATTICUS: It must have been disorderly. What did it consist of?

TOM: Got in a fight with another man, he tried to cut me.

ATTICUS: Did he succeed?

TOM: Yes suh, a little, not enough to hurt. You see, I–

ATTICUS: Yes, you were both convicted?

TOM: Yes suh, I had to serve 'cause I couldn't pay the fine. Other fellow paid his'n.

ATTICUS: Were you acquainted with Mayella Violet Ewell?

TOM: Yes suh, I had to pass her place goin' to and from the field every day.

ATTICUS: Whose field?

TOM: I picks for Mr. Link Deas.

ATTICUS: Were you picking cotton in November?

TOM: No suh, I works in his yard fall an' wintertime. I works pretty steady for him all year round, he's got a lot of pecan trees an' things.

ATTICUS: You say you had to pass the Ewell place to get to and from work. Is there any other way to go?

TOM: No suh, none's I know of.

ATTICUS: Tom, did she ever speak to you?

TOM: Why, yes, suh, I'd tip m' hat when I'd go by, and one day she asked me to come inside the fence and bust up a chiffarobe for her.

ATTICUS: When did she ask you to chop up the—the chiffarobe?

TOM: Mr. Finch, it was way last spring. I remember it because it was choppin' time and I had my hoe with me. I said I didn't have nothin' but this hoe, but she said she had a hatchet. She give me the hatchet and I broke up the chiffarobe. She said, "I reckon I'll hafta give you a nickel, won't I?" an' I said, "No ma'am, there ain't no charge." Then I went home. Mr. Finch, that was way last spring, way over a year ago.

ATTICUS: Did you ever go on the place again?

TOM: Yes, suh.

ATTICUS: When?

TOM: Well, I went lots of times.

ATTICUS: Under what circumstances?

TOM: Please, suh?

ATTICUS: Why did you go inside the fence lots of times?

TOM: She'd call me in, suh. Seemed like every time I passed by yonder, she'd have some little something for me to do—choppin', kindlin', totin' water for her. She watered them red flowers every day.

ATTICUS: Were you ever paid for your services?

TOM: No, suh, not after she offered me a nickel the first time. I was glad to do it. Mr. Ewell didn't seem to help her none, and neither did the chillun, and I knowed she didn't have no nickels to spare.

ATTICUS: Where were the other children?

TOM: They was always around, all over the place. They'd watch me work, some of 'em, some of 'em'd set in the window.

ATTICUS: Would Miss Mayella talk to you?

TOM: Yes, sir, she talked to me.

ATTICUS: Did you ever, at any time, go on the Ewell property—did you ever set foot on the Ewell property without an express invitation from one of them?

TOM: No, suh, Mr. Finch, I never did. I wouldn't do that, suh.

ATTICUS: Tom, what happened to you on the evening of November twenty-first of last year.

TOM: Mr. Finch, I was goin' home as usual that evenin', an' when I passed the Ewell place Miss Mayella were on the porch, like she said she were, it seemed real quiet like, an' I didn't quite know why. I was studyin' why, just passin' by, when she says for me to come there and help her a minute. Well, I went inside the fence an' looked around for some kindlin' to work on, but I didn't see none, and she says, "Naw, I got somethin' for you to do in the house. Th' old door's off its hinges an' fall's comin' on pretty fast." I said, "You got a screwdriver, Miss Mayella?" She said she sho' had. Well, I went up the steps an' she motioned me to come inside, and I went in the front room an' looked at the door. I said, "Miss Mayella, this door look all right." Then she shet the door in my face. Mr. Finch, I was wonderin' why it was so quiet like, an' it come to me that there weren't a chile on the place, not a one of 'em, and I said, "Miss Mayella, where the chillun? I say where the chillun'? An' she says to get ice creams. She says, "Took me a year to save seb'n nickels, but I done it. They all gone to town."

ATTICUS: What did you say then, Tom?

TOM: I said somehin' like, why, Miss Mayella, that's right smart o' you to treat 'em. An' she said, "You think so?" I don't think she understood what I was thinkin'—I meant it was smart of her to save like that, an' nice of her to treat em'.

ATTICUS: I understand you, Tom. Go on.

TOM: Well, I said I best be goin', I couldn't do nothin' for her, an' she says oh yes I could, an' I ask her what, and she says to just step on that chair yonder an' git that box down from on top of the chiffarobe.

ATTICUS: Not the same chiffarobe you busted up?

TOM: Naw, suh, another one. Most as tall as the room. So I done what she told me, an' I was just reachin' when the next thing I knows she—she'd grabbed me round the legs, grabbed me round th' legs, Mr. Finch. She scared me so bad I hopped down an' turned the chair over—that was the only thing, only furniture, 'sturbed in that room, Mr. Finch, when I left it. I swear 'fore God.

ATTICUS: What happened after you turned the chair over? (pause) Tom, you're sworn to tell the whole truth. Will you tell it? What happened after that?

JUDGE TAYLOR: Answer the question.

TOM: Mr. Finch, I got down offa that chair an' turned around an' she sorta jumped on me. ATTICUS: Jumped on you? Violently?

TOM: No, suh, she—she hugged me. She hugged me round the waist.

(Judge Taylor's gavel comes down with a bang.)

ATTICUS: Then what did she do?

TOM: She reached up an' kissed me' side of th' face. She says she never kissed a grown man before an' she might as well kiss a black man. She says what her papa do to her don't count. She says, "Kiss me back, black man." I say, "Miss Mayella, lemme outa here," an' tried to run but she got her back to the door an' I'da had to push her. I didn't wanta harm her, Mr. Finch, an' I say lemme pass, but just when I say it Mr. Ewell yonder hollered through th' window.

ATTICUS: What did he say?

TOM: Somethin' not fittin' to say—not fittin' for these foldks an' chillun to hear—

ATTICUS: Then what happened?

TOM: Mr. Finch, I was runnin' so fast I didn't know what happened.

ATTICUS: Tom, did you rape Mayella Ewell?

TOM: I did not, suh.

ATTICUS: Did you harm her in any way?

TOM: I did not, suh.

ATTICUS: Did you resist her advances?

TOM: Mr. Finch, I tried to 'thout bein' ugly to her. I didn't wanta be ugly, I didn't wanta push her or nothin'.

ATTICUS: Tom, go back once more to Mr. Ewell. Did he say anything to you?

TOM: Not anything, suh. He mighta said somethin', but I weren't there—

ATTICUS: That'll do. What you did hear, who was he talking to?

TOM: Mr. Finch, he were talkin' and lookin' at Miss Mayella.

ATTICUS: Then you ran?

TOM: I was scared, suh.

ATTICUS: Why were you scared?

TOM: Mr. Finch, if you was a black man like me, you'd be scared, too.

MR. LINK DEAS: I just want the whole lot of you to know one thing right now. That boy's worked for me eight years an' I ain't had a speck o' trouble outa him. Not a speck.

JUDGE TAYLOR: SHUT YOUR MOUTH, SIR! Link Deas, if you have anything you want to say, you can say it under oath and at the proper time, but until then you get out of this room, you hear me? Get out of this room, sir, you hear me? I'll be damned if I'll listen to this case again!

MR. GILMER: You were given thirty days once for disorderly conduct, Robinson?

TOM: Yes, suh.

MR. GILMER: What'd the black man look like when you got through with him?

TOM: He beat me, Mr. Gilmer.

MR. GILMER: Yes, but you were convicted, weren't you?

ATTICUS: It was a misdemeanor and it's in the record, Judge.

JUDGE TAYLOR: Witness'll answer, though.

MR. GILMER: Robinson, you're pretty good at busting up chiffarobes and kindling with one hand, aren't you?

TOM: Yes, suh, I reckon so.

MR. GILMER: Strong enough to choke the breath out of a woman and sling her to the floor?

TOM: I never done that, suh.

MR. GILMER: But you are strong enough to?

TOM: I reckon so, suh.

MR. GILMER: Had your eye on her a long time, hadn't you, boy?

TOM: No, suh, I never looked at her.

MR. GILMER: Then you were mighty polite to do all that chopping and hauling for her, weren't you, boy?

TOM: I was just tryin' to help her out, suh.

MR. GILMER: That was mighty generous of you. You had chores at home after your regular work, didn't you?

TOM: Yes, suh.

MR. GILMER: Why didn't you do them instead of Miss Ewell's?

TOM: I done 'em both, suh.

MR. GILMER: You must have been pretty busy. Why?

TOM: Why what, suh?

MR. GILMER: Why were you so anxious to do that woman's chores?

TOM: Looked like she didn't have nobody to help her, like I says—

MR. GILMER: With Mr. Ewell and seven children on the place, boy.

TOM: Well, I says it looked like they never help her none—

MR. GILMER: You did all this chopping and work from sheer goodness, boy?

TOM: Tried to help her, I says.

MR. GILMER: You're a mighty good fellow, it seems. Did all this for not one penny?

TOM: Yes, suh. I felt right sorry for her, she seemed to try mor'n the rest of 'em—

MR. GILMER: You felt sorry for her, you felt sorry for her? (long pause) Now, you went by the house as usual, last November twenty-first, and she asked you to come in and bust up a chiffarobe?

TOM: No, suh.

MR. GILMER: Do you deny that you went by the house?

TOM: No, suh. She said she had somethin' for me to do inside the house?

MR. GILMER: She says she asked you to bust up a chiffarobe, is that right?

TOM: No, suh, it ain't.

MR. GILMER: Then you say she's lying, boy?

TOM: I don't say she's lyin, Mr. Gilmer, I say she?s mistaken in her mind.

MR. GILMER: Didn't Mr. Ewell run you off the place, boy?

TOM: No, suh, I don't think he did.

MR. GILMER: Don't think, what do you mean?

TOM: I mean, I didn't stay long enough for him to run me off.

MR. GILMER: You're very candid about this. Why did you run so fast?

TOM: I says I was scared, suh.

MR. GILMER: If you had a clear conscience, why were you scared?

TOM: Like I says before, it weren't safe for any black person to be in a fix like that.

MR. GILMER: But you weren't in a fix. You testified that you were resisting Miss Ewell. Were you so scared that she'd hurt you? You ran, a big buck like you?

TOM: No, suh, scared I'd hafta face up to what I didn't do.

MR. GILMER: Are you being impudent to me, boy?

TOM: No, suh, I didn't mean to be.

(Mr. Tate takes Tom out of the court room and comes back in after the jury returns. The jury hands a paper to Judge Taylor.)

JUDGE TAYLOR: The jury finds Tom Robinson. Guilty, guilty, guilty, guilty!!!

STORYTELLING

JOANNE KILGOUR DOWDY

POETRY TO DRAMA

WHAT TO DO

— Read poem.
— Sketch poem: Beginning, middle and end frames of a storyboard.
— Share the sketch and story with a partner.
— Share the story from your poem with the big group.
— Write an "expression" based on the person who is being described in the poem, i.e., use the list generated in the writing workshop during the previous week.
— Share the expression with your buddy.
— Whole class discussion: what did you learn about the person in the poem? For example, who, what when, where and how did he or she come to have the experience in the poem?
— What did you learn about the person telling the story in the poem, if it is a story about someone else?

POEM SCRIPTS

1. What do you know about your character?
   Who, What, When, Where, Why, How?
2. What is the attitude of the character in this story/poem?
3. Pose in the attitude of your character. Play statues.
4. Pose with other characters in a tableau depicting a story.
5. Have your characters create a conversation with another person/attitude.
6. Write a play about the characters/attitudes that you are depicting using all the characters you have learned about through the stories/poems.
7. Rehearse your play.
8. Present your play to the big group.

J.K. Dowdy and S. Kaplan, Teaching Drama in the Classroom, 111–111.

JOANNE KILGOUR DOWDY

MOVIE SCRIPTS

INTRODUCTION

Teaching filmmaking helps students understand what they are offered on big, small and the computer screens (Farbman, 2005). They become skillful in asking questions about the purpose of sequential choices and how it can be represented off the screen or the page (Farbman). Students also learn how to find the most important sections of text, the storyline represented in the beginning, middle and end, and illustrate those sections as separate frames or images (Author, 2004).

When we tell writing students that a picture is "worth a thousand words," it is this way of looking at the world that makes a comic strip seem a natural extension of their writing tools. Becoming the "human projector" (Carrier, p. 56) that connects the shots in a comic strip makes engagement with the sequential art form an exciting game that students want to be involved in and claim as an experience. For many students it is the emphasis on image-making and interpreting images that relieves them of the often terrifying burden of using "correct" grammar, punctuation, sentence structure and story development (Bruce, 2004).

STEPS

— Instructor hands out storyboards and
— puts students in groups of three. Instructor tells students to choose a storyboard,
— then individually make up a beginning, middle and end to the story in the storyboard.

Example of one student's Beginning, Middle and End:

Beginning: Caspy is writing his autobiography. Mmmm ... he looks tasty. Let's split him – I get the leg.

Middle: Shaggy and Flopsy sneak up on Caspy. He sees them, says hi guys – wait a minute, I'm almost finished.

End: They wait patiently.

J.K. Dowdy and S. Kaplan, Teaching Drama in the Classroom, 113–118.

- Instructor hands out screenplays to look over and asks students to write down what they notice about how it's written:
  - Caps left align – setting (INT- or EXT-)
  - Right align (about five spaces from right margin): Camera directions (cut to, fade n to, etc.)
  - Character name: all caps, indented to center
  - Character lines underneath (indented to 15 spaces)
  - Front page – Title (Bold)
    By
    Name (centered, approx. 1 1/4" from top of page)
  - Page numbers upper right
  - Copyright symbol and year (© 2002) Approx 2" from bottom, left side
  - Name, Address, Phone directly across on right side
- Write a film script with group based on storyboard (15 minutes).
- Present to class as a staged reading while audience members close their eyes.
- Continue writing story individually in class and at home.

Steps to get you to final professional script:

1. Storyboard
2. Story grammar (Beginng, Middle, End)
3. Cut up frames/arrange in the order that makes the story flow.
4. Create characters: use who, what, when, where and why questions to fill in the autobiography of each character.
5. Develop setting: use your "inner eye" to fill out the details of the place/s where the action takes place. Be the "camera" that observe the details.
6. Read example scripts – decide on and list criteria/elements.

Materials: storyboards, samples, scissors, glue, large paper.

Expectations: Work cooperatively, time writing sequences, each person completes a component, chairs in a row for reading, audience closes eyes to visualize, respect the materials, applaud when others share. Remember, all the DRAFTS of each script is a work in progress. The details of the story improve as writers get feedback and HEAR their work come to life in the staged reading.

- Ads/magazines—cut out pictures, make story, glue, laminate: use for story plot diagram.
- Importance of details (camera angles, character emotions, facial expressions, etc.)
- Comic strips are good storyboard examples, easy to find and cheap to collect.

Movie workshop to sensitize students to camera shots and effects of lighting:

1. Show film clips and ask students, "What do you see?"
2. Replay scenes, approximately three, and ask students, "What do you need to see?"

These are the elements in the film clips that you want students to start identifying –

Reading Movies:

Characterization: what do you notice every time the character appears, i.e., sound, light, colors of costumes, camera angles, distance from other characters in a setting?

Lighting: who is the center of attention, and where is the light coming from?

Sound: what is audible, or where is silence obvious?

Perspectives: who is looking at the scene and from where, i.e., in the room, outside, upstairs, overhead?

Interpret camera shots by frames, i.e., close-up, medium, long shots.

Script/dialogue: who has the most lines, and why?

Costuming

Location: inside or outside setting?

Texture of the film: black/white; which color is prominent?

Samples of movie scripts that students created in class:

The Final Chapter
By
Christina Romell

© 2008 Christina Romell
1259 Westview Cir. SE
North Canton, OH 44720
330-966-2437

EXT- WOODS, LATE AFTERNOON

CU of Caspy writing on tree stump. Caspy is pale and bald with a big head, no ears and a very big nose. His tongue is sticking out the side of his mouth to show his intensity.

Pan out to MED shot of Shaggy and Flopsy sneaking up on Caspy. Shaggy (male) on right scoots as Flopsy (female) crouches.

CASPY: I just need to get this done!

Camera pans out to wider angle. Caspy feels breath on his neck. Startled, he turns around, drops his pencil.

CASPY: What do you want?

SHAGGY: We're so hungry. We want to eat you.

Caspy picks up his pencil.

CASPY: You can't eat me yet. I'm writing my autobiography.

Shaggy and Flopsy glance at each other.

FLOPSY: Hmmm ... Well, OK. I suppose we can wait.

They pull back slightly. Caspy goes back to writing. He says to himself ...

CASPY: ... and then these two big monsters came and wanted to eat me. I told them I was still working on my autobiography.

CUT TO:

EXT- CU of trees, night is falling. PAN out to MED shot of Flopsy, Shaggy, Caspy. Caspy is still writing furiously. Shaggy is tapping his toes. Flopsy is nodding off. Shaggy nudges her.

SHAGGY: OK, I think we've given him long enough.

Shaggy reaches out. Caspy trembles.

CUT TO:

CU of Caspy:

CASPY: Bbbut – I'm still not finished. If you're hungry, why don't you follow me? I will take you to my grammy's house. She makes great meatballs.

PAN OUT to MED shot. Caspy starts to back away slowly. Flopsy perks up.

FLOPSY: I love meatballs!

CU of Shaggy. He sighs heavily and purses his lips.

SHAGGY: Hooah ...

FADE TO:

INT-GRAMMY'S HOUSE-DAYTIME

Caspy, Flopsy and Shaggy sit around the kitchen table with napkins as bibs. Grammy is in the background in front of the stove. She wears an apron and stirs a pot that is steaming. There is a platter of steaming meatballs in the middle of the table. Caspy smiles as he watches his new friends enjoying their meal. Flopsy and Shaggy shovel meatballs into their mouths and nod their approval.

THE END

Jaclyn Consilio

CLYDE (in Chinese): You can't have my homework, I won't give it to you.

CUT TO:

PLUTO (pounding his fists): We can use force if you won't cooperate.

ZOOM TO HIS HANDS:

LONG SHOT OF A BIG DUST BOWL WITH ARMS/LEGS STICKING OUT

CLYDE: Gggggguys … stop really. I don't have YOUR homework.

ZOOM TO CLYDE WITH SCRAPES/BRUISES ON HIM AND JOCKS WIPING THEIR HANDS CLEAN:

CUT TO:

JAKE: We saw you today during lunch and told you your geometry homework better be finished by 4:30 PM and you were quite clear of the consequences.

PLUTO: Yeah, you knew the deal because you dropped your lunch and practically peed your pants. HAHAHAHA.

CUT TO:

CLYDE: Fellas, fellas, you are truly mistaken. That must've been my brother Cletus you were speaking with. Everyone knows I don't eat during lunch. I read books in the library.

ZOOM TO HEAD SHOT OF JAKE AND PLUTO WITH SURPRISED LOOKS:

PLUTO & JAKE: Where is he? Let us at 'em!!!

CUT TO:

CLYDE: Oh, Cletus is at glee club practice. You can find him there.

ZOOM OUT:

PLUTO & JAKE GO GALLOPING AWAY AS FAST AS THEY CAN.

HEAD SHOT OF CLYDE:

CLYDE: Too bad I don't even have a brother ... SUCKERS!!! HAHAHAHA!

CUT TO:

CLYDE SHOVES HIS HOMEWORK INTO HIS BAG AND SKIPS AWAY.

JACQUELINE PECK

FINDING STORIES WORTH TELLING

RATIONALE

This workshop was designed to model and engage classroom teachers in reviewing their family experiences to find stories worth telling in hopes that they
may support the students in their classrooms to do the same. Sharing our stories
helps us to honestly connect with others and to celebrate diversity by recognizing
both the similarities and differences in our stories. I first invited the teachers to
tell a story they likely knew quite well – the story of how they got their names.
After sharing these stories with peers, the students recognized how this process
enabled them to establish trust with each other. Indications of trust include teller-
listener eye contact during the story. Next I demonstrated ways to shape a memory
of a family member into a story by richly portraying the character, describing a
wounding event or crisis that forged changes in the character and relaying ways
the character used what s/he learned to resolve subsequent crises. Each student
then selected a character from her/his family and developed a story, which he
or she again shared in pairs. The students found that through their stories they
paid tribute to family members, uncovered memories and found some lessons
of value for themselves and others. I closed the workshop by demonstrating a
literature-storytelling connection with a jackdaw (e.g., a collection of artifacts
about a specific event, time or place) of my own family artifacts to tell the story of
my family's immigration to the United States. This jackdaw includes a book about
the European village my family left, my grandfather's passport, his citizenship
papers and photos taken at the time of their immigration.

WHAT TO DO

1. Model the process by telling the story of how you got your name.
2. Class members recall stories about how they got their names.
3. Class members share name stories with a peer and listen as peers share theirs.
4. Class reports on observations.
5. Model how to build a story around a memory of a family character. For example, describe one of your family members. Describe the setting in detail
   and use this person's phrases and gestures as you remember them. Describe
   an aspect of this person's character that shows a willingness to change and
   grow. Next describe a crisis event that caused your family member to change
   in some way. Then tell how this family member changed. Was there a change

J.K. Dowdy and S. Kaplan, Teaching Drama in the Classroom, 119–121.

in perspective? Some new learning? End your story by telling how this family member used the personal change to resolve other crises. What does this story "sound like"?

6. Class members choose family characters and use the framework to extend the memory into a story.
7. Class members tell their stories in small groups.
8. Class reports their observations, insights.
9. Create a jackdaw to accompany one of your family stories. Use the jackdaw to tell your personal story to make the event, time period or place come alive for your students.

   The table is a guide for creating a story about a family member, whether used with a jackdaw or not.
10. Guide your students to talk with their families about members who might become good stories. They may have artifacts to create a jackdaw and help tell the story.

SAMPLE

Character:	Grandmother Louise Scher
Set character in real world;	Born in 1906. Grew up in W. Virginia. Moved to Cleveland to attend Western Reserve College for Women (not sure of name – now Case).
Show someone able to grow and change;	Grandma was very strong-willed.
Use authentic language and mannerisms.	At age 20, married a man 20 years her senior. Lived in Shaker Heights. Husband was a Jewish immigrant from Russia. Parents didn't approve. They eloped.
	Husband was hard to live with, i.e., didn't want television in house. My grandmother (who had a job at G.E. teaching consumers how to use new stoves and ovens) bought a TV with her income. My grandfather left the house for three days.
	My grandfather died when she was in her early 50s. Grandma never remarried.
	Became very involved in Herb Society of Cleveland and Plymouth Church in Shaker. She led the women's fellowship for years. Grandma was a bit of a "know-it-all."

	At holidays when family gathered, we often played board games. Trivial Pursuit was a favorite. Grandma never played but she hovered, answering all the questions out loud. Always claimed how "easy" that was. We used to tease her that she sounded like Miss Piggy saying, "I knew that!"
Crisis or Wounding Event: What happens to change your character's view of the world?	At age 91 Grandma left Shaker to live in Hamlet Hills retirement community in Chagrin Falls near my family. (My Dad was her son. His only sister lives in Baltimore.) Very independent until one evening after driving herself home from our house she drove through her parking lot and into the woods near her apartment where she parked the car. Not hurt in any way, but clueless that anything was wrong. Worrying about her safety (as well as others on the road) my dad took away her keys and eventually sold her car.
Lessons Learned: How is your character a different, perhaps stronger, person? What does your character understand now that s/he didn't understand before the crisis?	Grandma never forgave my dad. In the next couple of years she went from her own apartment to assisted living to the manor where she eventually died at age 96.
Application: How does your character use the new understanding to face and resolve new crises?	

SUSAN V. IVERSON AND RHONDA S. FILIPAN

SCRIPTING SUCCESS: USING DIALOGUE WRITING TO HELP STUDENTS FIND THEIR VOICE

RATIONALE

With dropout rates as high as 25% for many first-year college students, retention is a key university initiative. Tinto (2005) asserts that students need both social and academic integration into the university community in order to be retained. However, even those students who persist to graduate-level studies are not immune to "stopping out" or "dropping out" of school. For instance, the pursuit of doctoral degrees is often described in terms of survival, and a look at completion rate data suggests why. The attrition rate in Ph.D. programs in the U.S. is as high as 50% (Smallwood, 2004). While doctoral study may be erroneously viewed as the completion of a series of courses and writing a dissertation, it is as much, if not more so, about self-authorship – "a complex blend of autonomy and connection" (Rogers et al., in Baxter Magolda & King, p. 213).

Our aim as educators is to support students' learning to author their own perspectives, regardless of their academic level: secondary school, undergraduate or graduate study. One strategy by which to help students make sense of their experience and begin to self-author is through story-telling, or more specifically as we describe here, scripting one's experiences in dialogue: "Although a life is not a narrative, people make sense of their lives and the lives of others through narrative constructions" (Richardson, 1990, p. 10). Inviting students to write a script of their experience enables students to convey what is important, (re)arranging and (re)stating events to prepare for a narrative climax. It is, Wright tells us, "retrospective, in effect making a case" and may be "ambiguously authored ... composed by a mediator who arranges the testimony and quietly supplies explanatory interventions" (in Reinharz, p. 130). Thus, the authoring of oneself through story-telling provides a space for understanding (Munro, 1998).

Students learn that success in their studies typically means finding one's unique voice and having the courage both to *assert* that voice and to *insert* it into the discourse of the discipline. What makes this feat especially difficult for students at all levels is the cacophony of competing voices that drown out their own: advisors and guidance counselors, the dissertation chair, peer groups, teachers and faculty, and well-intentioned family and friends.

Research focusing on students' intellectual development traces a progression from dualistic thinking, to an appreciation of multiplicity of views including one's own voice, to relativism, where the objectivity of an academic discipline is respected as a way of knowing – not simply adopted but recognized as constructed knowledge (Baxter Magolda, 2001; King & Kitchener, 1994; Perry, 1970). In a similar vein, Gilligan's research on adolescent girls describes the often difficult process of finding one's true, emerging voice while ignoring and squelching the "false feminine" voices.

Scholars, like Gilligan and others, have noted that gender distinctions in intellectual development exist. In *Women's Ways of Knowing*, the authors describe the significance of subjective knowledge to women's development. Here the woman has made a breakthrough from being *recipient* of knowledge to viewing herself as a *source* of knowledge (Belenky, Clinchy, Goldberger, & Tarule, 1997). These scholars illuminate how students – men *and* women – may not yet see themselves as co-creators of knowledge. Doctoral students, in particular, may not yet have the developmental capacity to find their voice, making self-authorship unlikely and completion of the Ph.D. program potentially impossible. Writing exercises, in the form of scripts and dialogues, may help facilitate these cognitive shifts.

STEPS

Instructors increasingly assign reflective writing as a tool for enabling students at all educational levels to think about their experiences (i.e., assigned readings, in-class discussions) and to make connections between those experiences and other content, contexts and settings. In this way, students increase their capacity for critical consciousness, the development of "personal awareness, and scrutiny of certain aspects of identity previously taken for granted" (Jones & Abes, 2004, p. 149; also Eyler & Giles, 1999; Rosenberger, 2000).

Richardson (1990) asks what strategies we can use to write the lives of people so that our writing matters. In response, we propose the use of script writing and dialogue writing as a curricular strategy to help students write their lives. More specifically, the use of drama in education can be used to help students make sense and meaning of their educational experiences and to "stage" their performance. Writing scripts and dialogues may allow students to give voice to powerful emotions. Furthermore, writing these dialogues and scenarios (real and imagined) may lead students to enhanced self-awareness, finding and empowering one's voice and potentially an increased rate of educational completion, be it a high school diploma, undergraduate degree, or even a Ph.D. Thus, script and dialogue writing could be a tool to combat student attrition at all levels and to discover one's authentic voice.

An instructor or advisor/mentor seeking to use such a pedagogical approach may suggest the following writing prompts as journal activities:

- Write a script/dialogue in which your *heart* and your *head* speak to each other.

  - For High School Students: How does your heart feel about your high school life? Your post-high school plans? What do family members wish (or expect) for your future? What does your head think about these same things? Who are YOU listening to: your heart or your head?

- For Doctoral Students: How does your *heart* feel about your dissertation topic? Your research methodology? Your doctoral program of study? Your career goals? And what does your *head* think about these choices? Is one side winning ... or are they both just talking at this point?

— Write a script/dialogue in which you speak with another student or class-mate: someone you admire, someone for whom you have envy, someone who intimidates you, or someone who makes you angry. What would you say to this person?

— Write a script/dialogue in which your *academic and scholarly self* (the one who takes classes and goes to school) speaks to another dimension of your-self: the student athlete, the parent, the employee, the boyfriend/girlfriend, the spouse, the son/daughter, the friend, the lover, the caregiver. What would your *scholarly self* say to this *other self*? How, in turn, would this *other self* respond? You may even want to script three or more dimensions of yourself engaging in a conversation!

— Write a script/dialogue in which you speak to an important person in your academic life (i.e., your guidance counselor, your advisor, your dissertation chair). What would you say about your concerns, your fears, your academic goals, your program of study, your dissertation topic ... your hopes and dreams? The first draft could be a monologue of all the things you'd *really* like to say to this important person in your academic life. In the second draft, you can then add that person's (anticipated or ideal) responses, switching to a dialogue. This exercise can be further adapted to add more voices and perspectives.

- For High School and Undergraduate Students: Imagine yourself as a holo-gram, one of those 3-D images (sometimes on book covers or bookmarks) that changes if someone tilts the object in a different direction. When people *first* look at you, who is the person they always see? How does that image shift and change as you move the hologram? What are the hidden parts of yourself in your hologram, the ones not visible at first glance? Script a conversation between those different aspects of yourself.

- For Doctoral Students: Imagine taking yourself out for a bite to eat and engaging in a conversation with yourself – you in *years past* (before grad-uate school), you in *the present* (in the midst of doctoral study) and you in *the future* (with a Ph.D. in hand and working at your dream job). What would these three characters say to each other? What questions would be asked? What advice would the characters give each other, and what feedback would each need to receive? What insights would be shared?

After soliciting an initial draft for any of the above topics, instructors may follow up with the activities below:

- Arrange students in small groups with peers, inviting them to share reactions to each other's work, pose questions about the script and solicit feedback from group members.
- Use the peer review of writing strategy: One student may be assigned to read another student's script and write a response, inserting him/herself into the dialogue.
- Ask the author of the original dialogue to add additional voices (at least a third voice) to the piece and even to alter the names and characteristics of the characters in the evolving script.
- Ask students to interview others (peers, advisor, instructor, family) about educational events and then incorporate the others' points of view into one's life story or script.
- Encourage students to revise their script (adding, deleting or changing lines) by taking into account the feedback from their peer reviewers.
- Invite students to perform their scripts or direct peers in a performance.
- Suggest that students write a one-page reflective essay on strengths and limitations of script-writing.
- Facilitate a classroom discussion in which students talk about how script writing – and reading the scripts of others – enabled them to confront feelings.

Through narrative, students are (re)organizing their experiences into temporally meaningful episodes (Polkinghorne, 1988). As Richardson (1990) notes, "The meaning of each event is produced by its temporal position and role in a comprehensive whole ... The connections between the events is the meaning" (p. 21).

SAMPLES

To illustrate this script-writing process, we offer two examples from our doctoral experiences. Learning in this research-intensive environment rewards objectivity rather than self-examination, and we were challenged to find our voice. For Rhonda, script-writing was a self-assigned exercise, helping her gain insight into her relationship with research. Susan was assigned in a doctoral class to develop an intellectual autobiography over the course of the semester and found script-writing to be an appealing format.

First, we offer an excerpt from Rhonda's journal in which she created a dialogue with Research, a character scripted as a man. Doing so enabled her to explore the role of research in her life – as a doctoral student now and in the future.

Rhonda: I was so smitten with you when we met a few years ago in *Quantitative Methods I*. Do you remember how nervous I was? All those numbers! I couldn't stop thinking about you. I'd never met anyone like you before in my life. You kept me up late at night, you know ...
Research: Lies, lies, lies. All of it.

126

Rhonda: No, it isn't. I mean it. I was so thrilled to learn about you and all your complexity, all your nuances, all your methods. I liked hearing about your friendships with the epistemologies, too. I loved getting to know the differences between linear regression and grounded theory, between multivariate analysis and phenomenology. You're deep, R. You really are.

Research: So I've been told. But it's not enough for you?

Rhonda: [Sighs] No. It's not enough. If I look way down into myself, I know that our relationship will eventually reach an end point. This is going to sound harsh, but I just don't see you in my future.

Research: Gee, thanks for notifying me. So what about all the projects and papers we've done together so far? What about the two proposals we're writing this term? Not to mention the five "Methods" classes I was a huge part of. Were you faking it?

Rhonda: No, I enjoyed every moment of every one of those things. Really. And I'll always treasure the classes, the papers, the projects. Those are great memories. It's just that I don't want to do those things forever, R. It's not me. I'm caught somewhere between conventional and creative. I don't know quite where I'll fit in, to be honest.

Research: Well, what about the big trip we've been planning. To Dissertation?

Rhonda: I can't wait for that! I'm so looking forward to it. I've already started to pack: my problem statement, my research question, some of the literature review, a couple pieces of the methods, and the theoretical framework, which is too big to fit in the suitcase at this point. But it's going to be an amazing journey, R. It's a destination that I've always wanted to go to ... and it's a trip that I'll remember forever. I'm really excited about it, and everyone says that I light up when I describe it.

Research: So let me get this straight. I excite you, but you're just going to *use* me to get to Dissertation, and then you're going to dump me?

By imagining Research as a man whom she *loves* but isn't *in love with* and by scripting a conversation with him, Rhonda was able to confront her ambiguous feelings about research, leading to deeper insight about its place in her life.

Second, we provide an excerpt from Susan's intellectual autobiography, in which she introduced several characters so that the story was "ambiguously authored" (Wright, in Richardson, p. 103). By telling the story through the voices of others, the result was not to find a unified story but a multiplicity of stories.

Scene I

The lights come up on three women sitting around a table in a conference room. Each has papers in her hands. More papers and notebooks are on the table. There are cups on the table and coffee is brewing.

Marilyn (*a voluptuous woman, who could have just walked off the cover of a fashion magazine*): Why did I take this job? We're never going to write a script of this woman's life. We've been at this for hours already and we can't agree on who she is, much less get the first words onto paper.

Rosie (*a woman dressed in coveralls who looks like she just walked off a construction site*): You sure are dimwitted there, Blondie. This script doesn't have to be so complicated, but I can see why it is a stretch for you. How did you even get this job?

Marilyn: How did *I* get this job? How did *you*? I can't imagine you're even literate. And don't call me Blondie!

Gloria (*a conservatively dressed woman, hair pulled up in a bun, wearing glasses*): Hey! (*interrupting them*) Can we try to focus? We have a big task ahead of us, and we're not making any progress arguing with each other. Let's review what we're supposed to be doing. The producer has asked us to write the play about Susan Iverson, her life story. It needs to be an account of her educational experiences and intellectual development. Now, all we've been doing is arguing about why we're here and what each other does or doesn't have to offer. Perhaps there is a reason we've been selected for this task, but at this point I think we have to set those speculations aside.

Rosie: And what do you propose we do then?

Gloria: I propose that we start with some interviews of key people in her life. This will inform our script writing. Does anyone have a better idea? (*pause*) Hearing none, let's start interviewing. I've invited a couple of her teachers to meet with us.

This dialogue between Marilyn, Rosie and Gloria allowed Susan to gain deeper insight into her intellectual development, enabled metacognitive reflections on her evolving epistemology and empowered her understanding of her role, and that of others, in knowledge construction.

In sum, creating dialogues and scripts can enable students to hear their own voice and to put it center stage in the spotlight, banishing the competing voices to a distant place—behind the curtain and offstage where they belong.

REFERENCES

Baxter Magolda, M. (2001). *Making their own way: Narratives for transforming higher education to promote self-development.* Sterling, VA: Stylus Publishers.
Baxter Magolda, M. & King, P. M. (eds.) (2004). *Learning partnerships: Theory and models of practice to educate for self-authorship.* Sterling, VA: Stylus Publishers.
Belenky, M. F., Clinchy, B. M., Goldberger, N. R., & Tarule, J. M. (1997). *Women's ways of knowing: The development of self, voice, and mind.* Basic Books.
Eyler, J. & Giles, Jr., D. E. (1999). *Where's the learning in service-learning?* San Francisco, CA: Jossey-Bass.
Gilligan, C. (1982). *In a different voice: Psychological theory and women's development.* Cambridge, MA: Harvard University Press.
Jones, S. R. & Abes, E. S. (2004). Enduring influences of service-learning on college students' identity development. *Journal of College Student Development, 45*(2), 149–166.
King. P. M. & Kitchener, K. S. (1994). *Developing reflective judgment: Understanding and promoting intellectual growth and critical thinking in adolescents and adults.* San Francisco, CA: Jossey-Bass.

Munro, P. (1998). *Subject to fiction: Women teachers' life history narratives and the cultural politics of resistance*. Philadelphia: Open University Press.

Perry, W. G. (1970). *Forms of intellectual and ethical development in the college years: A scheme*. Troy, MO: Holt, Rinehart, and Winston.

Polkinghorne, D. E. (1988). *Narrative knowing and the human sciences*. Albany: State University of New York Press.

Reinharz, S. (1992). *Feminist methods in social research*. NY: Oxford University Press.

Richardson, L. (1990). *Writing strategies: Reaching diverse audiences*. Sage.

Rosenberger, C. (2000). Beyond empathy: Developing critical consciousness through service-learning. In C. R. O'Grady (ed.), *Integrating service-learning and multicultural education in colleges and universities* (pp. 23–43). Mahwah, NJ: Lawrence Erlbaum Associates.

Tinto, V. (2005). *College student retention: Formula for student success*. Westport, CT: Praeger Publishers.

JOANNE KILGOUR DOWDY

LET'S HEAR IT: DRAMA AND RADIO

RATIONALE

This workshop was created to give students a chance to use newspapers and dialogue, combined with their dramatic skills, in a formal reading and writing context. When I found out that most of my pre-service teachers did not receive or read the daily newspapers, in hard copy or on the internet, I decided to integrate the use of newspapers into my literacy workshop. Sharing a collection of newspapers with my students, having them choose interesting articles to put in their personal portfolios, and then finding articles to give to each other based on a person's stated interest or persuasion, helped my students develop a practical approach to the inclusion of the daily newspapers in their classroom instructional practices. The collection of articles allowed students to get to know each other as they shared their findings and presented them as gifts to each other when they met for class.

WHAT TO DO

1. Participants brainstorm about forms of drama that they use in instruction.
2. The instructor asks participants to think about ways that they have engaged their students in learning about current events and share their ideas with the class.
3. Participants form groups.
4. Group members read the newspaper for an article of interest; members may need to combine a few articles to tell one story.
5. Groups decide on the characters to be scripted in a radio drama.
6. They sketch three frames for story: beginning, middle and end.
7. They create a script of two to three minutes following the above frames.
8. Groups rehearse the script for dramatic flow.
9. They record the script on audio tapes.
10. They share the audio recordings and written script with the class.
11. The class makes suggestions for future development, i.e., to add a scene before or afterward, to put more events in the present script, to add more characters from other articles in the newspaper.

J.K. Dowdy and S. Kaplan, Teaching Drama in the Classroom, 131–132.

SAMPLE

Charlie and the Chest's Talent
Ashley, Sarah and Aubrey

Narrator: Charlie Frye goes to the beach during the off-season to relax. Not realizing that it's a nude beach, Charlie Frye settles down on the sand when all of a sudden he spots a cedar chest washing ashore. He rushes after it. However, at the same time the nude native also sees the chest and runs in the same direction. Labeled on the chest are the words "caution: talent inside."

Charlie Frye: Yo, man, this talent could really be useful in taking my team to the Super Bowl.

Nudist: No way. I'm a Steelers fan, and I'm not letting you have this talent because we are gonna be the champs this year, again, and you will lose again, as always.

Chest: Now, now, don't argue. We can solve this peacefully. Charlie Frye will get the talent because the Browns need it more than the Steelers. It's only fair that we try to even out the playing field.

Nudist: Yeah, what now sucker?

Narrator: Not satisfied with the chest's conclusion, the nudist grabs the chest and makes a dash for it. Charlie Frye tackles him to the ground, the chest breaks open and Charlie gets the talent, meaning the Browns move on to a Super Bowl victory.

End of Scene

GOOD IDEAS

STEVEN L. TURNER

THE SKIN WE ARE IN: NAMING, SHARING AND EXPRESSING OURSELVES

Small Group and Whole Class Performance Poems

Suggested grade levels: 6th grade-adult

INTRODUCTION

When students enter classrooms for the first time, they are full of questions: "What will I learn here? What is this teacher like? Who are these people in the desks next to me?" Since students are especially curious about each other at the beginning of the school year, the first days of school offer an important opportunity to establish a sense of community and identity in the classroom. This chapter describes *Name Poems*, a student-centered activity that combines drama and writing with performance while giving students (and teachers) an opportunity to learn about each other. I initially developed this activity for a sixth-grade class and later adapted it for both an eighth-grade class and first-year college students.

DESCRIPTION OF ACTIVITIES: NAME POEMS

Rationale

This activity helps students learn names, introduces students to one another, encourages active class participation and honors student diversity.

Materials needed: pencil, paper (8 ½ × 11), poster board, colored markers, crayons.

PROCEDURE

1. Ask students to write their names in large colorful, bold letters at the top of their papers.
2. Explain to students they are to create a poem of four to ten lines that includes their names and several lines that share something about who they are, what their life is like or what is important to them. Explain to students the rationale for the activity. The number of lines in the poem can be adjusted to grade level or individual learners.
3. Remind students their name poems need not rhyme and that the words in their poems should be bold and descriptive, since they will have an opportunity to read their poem aloud. Ask students to underline or CAPITALIZE words that they want to emphasize when reading aloud.

J.K. Dowdy and S. Kaplan, Teaching Drama in the Classroom, 135–137.

4. It will be helpful for students if instructors model a few name poems:

Benjamin, 6th grade

My name is BEN
I am 12, not ten
I have a RED bike and a BLUE bike
Here are some things that I like
Drag racing
Skateboarding
Riding a bike too,
I'm excited to be in Mrs. McConnell's class this year
How about YOU?

Alicia, 8th grade

Alicia, Alicia, ALICIA,
I'm in the eighth grade
I'm one year closer to high school
I feel like throwing a PARADE!

Juliet, first-year college student

You can call me Julie
But Juliet is my name
I am NOT looking for Romeo
I'm looking for ME
I'm looking to LEARN
I'm looking to SEE
I'm looking to discover who I am
And create who it is I will be
So that's me
I'm Julie,
But Juliet is only my NAME
Who I am is up to ME

Steven, instructor, workshop for adults

My name is Steven
six letters, yes
but not JUST a word
My name can make me STAND up in a crowded room
Or lure me onto a plane or bus
My name can make me hide
or smile
and laugh
or sing
what is your name
what does YOUR name mean to you?

5. Once students have created their poems, ask them to get into groups of two or three and exchange poems. Practice reading the poems aloud to each other to prepare for whole-class presentation. Ask students to offer gentle, constructive suggestions to peers.

6. The activity concludes with whole-class reading of name poems. Students are encouraged to read their work with enthusiasm and engagement, to live the words and use their time to tell the name story they have created. Remind students to place special emphasis on the CAPITALIZED words in their poems.

7. Instructors may wish to encourage students to recreate their name poem on large posters and display them on a community bulletin board or wall.

SUGGESTED MODIFICATIONS AND ACCOMMODATIONS

— Create a partially completed name poem template to support struggling writers.

— Allow students to use a dictionary or thesaurus to brainstorm bold and descriptive words.

— Allow students who prefer not to present to the class the option to pass on the presentation part of the activity.

— Some students may prefer to create their name poems on a computer to integrate clip artwork, color and graphics.

CONCLUSION

Names are a significant part of people's identity. Participating in a Name Poem activity helps students develop affirmation and affiliation and supports cohesion of the class or group. This activity combines elements of drama, writing and performance with the goal of introducing students to each other. Name poems help to establish a setting for contribution and consistent partnerships in the class by giving students an opportunity to learn about each others' lives.

CAROL L. ROBINSON, DANIEL-RAYMOND NADON & NANCY M. RESH

A LESSON FOR MERGING POPULATIONS

The activity below is born of the tryout sessions for a performance project during Fall 2009. We wished to allow both hearing and Deaf students the opportunity to intermingle and struggle with the obstacles of communication in creatively expressive ways – to explore the contact zone between Deaf and hearing cultures. We chose a play that was intended for both hearing and Deaf American audiences (to be either simultaneously expressed in both spoken English and American Sign Language or in either one of these languages only). Students were partnered for like-roles (one hearing, one Deaf for each line expressed in the play). The challenge was to have them perform simultaneously in these two different languages, yet also individually so that it was clear that neither was interpreting for the other. One activity involved using no language at all – just gestures and pantomime. This activity allowed for an equal "playing ground" upon which all could build more sophisticated language use together. (Note: To prevent confusion over the directions, we had an interpreter helping us.) Thus, the goal of this exercise is to merge populations in an equitable manner that allows for evaluation of basic acting skills.[1]

MIME WARM-UP

This exercise allows students to work on and demonstrate skills in

- facial and bodily expression,
- mime ability,
- the ability to take emotional/expressive risks.

Steps

1. Bring half of the actors to the stage.

---

[1] One exercise, "Devil on My Shoulder," did not work for the goals of this project. In this exercise, one actor was asked to speak while a second actor was asked to sign: they were to look at each other and attempt to "voice" each other's subtext. The goal was to practice mixing voicing with signing in a synchronic performance fashion, but it was too much of a challenge at this early stage. We found that allowing actors to learn their lines in their particular language (spoken English or signed ASL) first, then to develop a performance of those lines, and finally to merge performances together was a more effective lesson.

J.K. Dowdy and S. Kaplan, Teaching Drama in the Classroom, 139–143.
© 2011 *Sense Publishers. All rights reserved.*

2. Explain that they will mime several suggestions (each for 30 seconds).
3. The second group of actors remains in their seats to watch carefully.
4. Give the first group of actors a few suggestions to mime "qualities" or states of being (i.e., anger, perkiness, frustration, embarrassment, etc.).
5. Switch and do the same for the second group of actors.
6. Switch back to the first group, but this time, instead of performing a "state of being," give them action to mime (searching for money, counting the seats in the auditorium, deciding who the three tallest people in the room are, etc.). Switch to the second group and repeat the exercise.
7. Discuss the differences between miming abstract concepts verses action. For example, they might discuss the ways in which performing a state of being, without a corresponding action often appears stereotypical, forced, false, while performing an action is more complex, natural and true.

PLACE-TO-PLACE

Start in one place (such as a car) and transfer to another (such as cooking in the kitchen). This exercise allows exploration of

- mime ability,
- specific physical communication skills,
- specific facial communication skills.

Steps

1. Ask the actors to select two related locations and activities (i.e., kitchen, eating breakfast; and bathroom, brushing teeth).
2. Instruct actors to work up a silent mime wherein they move from one activity to another.
3. In connecting the two ordinary tasks, challenge them to think outside the box. For example:

   - moving from breakfast to brushing teeth
   - one might notice an "accident" from the family dog, clean it up, and stub her/his toe in the process
   - putting on a bandage but pausing to talk on the phone
   - washing the dishes and noticing something happening out the window (above the sink)
   - moving from driving a car to going inside a building and talking with a colleague in the hallway
   - moving from working on the computer to reading a book and to be as specific as possible.

4. Place actors in a circle and provide an example for them to emulate. (This is done typically by selecting a talented student or by the teacher her/himself.) Ask for volunteers to begin.

5. Observe their clarity, specificity and imagination. At the end of each actor's turn,

   a) Ask others to guess the two activities.
   b) Look for examples in which the actor can be more specific, clear or imaginative.
   c) Have other actors provide positive reinforcement, explaining why the choices worked.

US VS. THEM

In this exercise students are divided into two groups – one speaking, one signing – and they are asked to "one-up" the other group through expressive language (acting with language). This exercise allows students to explore and demonstrate

- interpersonal communication skills,
- spoken/signed language skills (articulation through spoken English and/or signed ASL),
- listening through hearing/watching skills,
- the concept of "build" and "status" ("I'm better than you and, therefore . . . ").

Steps

1. Divide the group into two smaller groups, hearing vs. deaf.
2. Suggest that each group take turns proving through language (English and ASL) that they are the coolest, toughest, meanest, most powerful group.
3. As the one group performs (for 30 seconds), the other group watches carefully and plans to aim bigger, meaner, etc. when it is their turn to compete.
4. Each team takes a turn until a group fails to "top" the other team.
5. While they compete, the instructor side-coaches that they should

   a) use their imagination in creating status, rather than just getting "bigger";
   b) work well together as a team and not "preen";
   c) learn to examine the other group's behavior and "top" it;
   d) be specific in their physical expression.

GESTURE AND MIME COMMUNICATION

This exercise involves two people. One person is given a piece of paper with a statement and tries to communicate the statement without using spoken words or sign language. The second person must try to understand what the first person is saying. This exercise develops

- non-verbal/non-signed communication skills,
- mime skills,

— chemistry between the two actors.

Steps

1. Prepare several statements that could be difficult to mime (we used the text of *For Every Man, Woman, and Child* – a modern morality play inspired by EVERYMAN (by Willy Conley)). For example:
   - "Beauty is in the eye of the beholder"
   - "The meek shall inherit the earth"
   - "A cat on a hot tin roof"
   - "Give me liberty or give me death"
   - "To be or not to be"
   - "A kingdom for a horse!"
   - Demonstrate an example, asking the full group to guess what you are doing.
2. Call for volunteers and create a line-up to begin.
3. Work your way through the line, allowing each student a chance to mime her/his "line" (one of the statements handed out above) to the group. As each student works, side coaching may be necessary or helpful.
4. Side-coaching may include the following instructions:
   a) Be more specific.
   b) Here is something to try (give suggestions).
   c) Start with the noun (or verb).
5. If the second individual is unable to guess the statement, stop the action, disclose the answer and work together as a group to come up with an effective mime.

I AM THE ABSTRACT

Each student is asked to "be" a god or goddess (such as Jesus, Ra or Zeus) or to be an allegorical figure (Good Deeds, Death, Beauty, Judgment). Students are challenged to physicalize or personify abstract beings or allegorical figures. This is an exercise for development of movement and facial expression skills.

Steps

1. Give each actor a piece of paper with an allegorical figure or god or goddess on it, and instruct them not to disclose what is on it.
2. Form two lines, the first line facing the second line, with a large playing area between them.
3. The actor at the front of each line will enter the playing area and mime a "meeting" or "confrontation" with another based on the assigned character and the character approaching him or her. The exercise continues until each character in group 1 has "met" most of the characters in group 2.

4. Upon the completion of the exercise, the lines are formed again. This time the actors are able to use language in their "meeting" (with interpreters present and translating). Once again, allow each character in group 1 to "meet" most of the characters in group 2.

5. Upon the completion of that exercise, the lines are formed again. This last time the actors must "meet" again but work to communicate without an interpreter, whether or not they use the same language.

MARY E. WEEMS

DON'T BE AFRAID TO FLY: USING DRAMA TO INSPIRE SELF-ESTEEM

Ten years ago I created the F.L.Y. (Finding Love in Yourself) Girl Workshop to help high school girls discover the power of their own beauty. Using my own life as an example, I realized that I spent many years of my youth looking for love in all the wrong places, including the wrong men, the wrong job and self-destructive behaviors, because I didn't love myself. No one had ever spoken to me about self-esteem, but it wasn't until I became aware of it in my early 30s through an article in *Essence Magazine* that I started the long journey toward becoming the person I am today.

I had the privilege of facilitating the workshop as part of Ohio University's Upward Bound program from 2004 through 2009. I used oral improvisation, prompted dramatic writings, objects, costuming, music, drawing, visual images, movement and meditation to help each girl discover the beautiful butterfly hiding under the cocoon of low self-esteem, shaped by lived experiences including exposure to a media that tells them they're imperfect, un-attractive and too fat.

Each workshop began with my explanation of the butterfly metaphor and the stages of development girls (like butterflies) go through. I explained that too many of us get stuck in the cocoon stage, inhibiting our ability to break free of self-loathing, recover through a healing process and develop the love that sustains any woman who learns to live fully alive and aware in the world.

Out of all the activities, nothing was more revelatory than when the girls had the opportunity to participate in creating their own short writings and bring them to life in a small space in a traditional classroom that became the stage for their powerful words.

PROCEDURE

1. Ask the girls to meditate using either Nature Sound CDs or jazz music, for example, Miles Davis' "My Funny Valentine." The music should be from seven to ten minutes long. Here's how to facilitate the meditation:

   — Ask participants to sit in a comfortable position in their chairs, keeping their eyes closed until instructed to open them.
   — Ask the girls to take three deep, cleansing breaths with you.

J.K. Dowdy and S. Kaplan, Teaching Drama in the Classroom, 145–147.

- Next, ask them to listen closely to the music while repeating a single word they like over and over. Word suggestion: Love.
- When the music ends, ask them to open their eyes and write about an unforgettable memory. Time: 5 minutes.
- Let girls who would like to share these writings as a way of beginning the session. It's a warm-up for their creative muscles.

2. Ask each girl to make a list of topics she'd like to explore through drama. Popular topics include relationships with mother, father, relationships with boys or girls their age, drug and alcohol use among family members or boys and girls their age, and sexual assault.
3. Talk about the power of dramatic writing and performance, sharing several short examples. There are numerous age-specific titles available. Two I've used are *Multicultural Monologues for Young Actors*, edited by Craig Slaight and Jack Sharrar, and *Teen Talk: Modern Monologues for Teenage Girls* by Susan Pomerance.
4. Place a selection of prompts around the room to provide variety including visual images, objects, hats and other costuming. The images should all be pertinent to young girls; for example, popular magazine images of girls and young women in various settings, including magazine ads, newspaper images of girls and women in real life settings and ads, history-of-women cards with images of famous women on the front and autobiographical information on the back all work well. I recommend putting together a collection of things to use for this project.
5. Give one to three writing-specific prompts and give the girls ten minutes for each writing to create drafts. Sample writing prompts: What is the woman in the image thinking? Write about an unforgettable memory. How do you define a woman?
6. Break the girls into small groups and ask them to share their writings out loud.
7. Ask each group to share one or more of the writings with the class from the stage space.
8. Discuss the work, making suggestions for improving the original draft.
9. Ask each group to work on turning one of the writings into a scene to be shared the next day.
10. Allow time for each group to share their scene, and then discuss possibilities for a final draft, including finding venues for sharing the scene when they return to their home communities.

Sample: David's Gift, by Sarah

Prompt: An unforgettable memory

(Girls stand in a circle with their backs to the center to reflect their "one" character. The circle rotates so that each time a girl speaks she is facing the audience.)

Girl 1: When I was a little girl I was quiet and shy. I was ugly, too dark, too fat, and I couldn't talk right.

Girl 2: I could be standing right beside you, and you wouldn't notice until I was gone.

Girl 3: I tried to be understood by someone, anyone. I didn't want to share my whole self, just a piece of me.

Girl 1: Life went on and I became a wallflower. I talked, but very low – I

Girl 2: ... let people walk all over me, and I didn't care.

Girl 3: Then one day –

Girl 1: ... all of that changed – I met David. He was nice, with blonde curly hair, blue eyes and a white smile that would last for days.

Girl 2: I was in second grade. I was in love! I could talk to him freely. He listened and never called me names.

Girl 3: I felt different from the other kids and so did he.

Girl 1: He lived in a trailer and always wore old clothes that didn't fit him right.

Girl 2: We became best friends for a year.

Girl 3: We held hands, we talked, we kissed on the cheek.

Girl 1: One day he said, "Sarah, I got you something."

Girl 2: I waited all day and when school was out, I convinced my sister to walk home without me.

Girl 3: I sat there waiting while the other kids walked, took the bus, or got picked up.

Girl 1: Just as I stood up to walk home, I heard David call my name.

Girl 2: I turned to look for him but –

Girl 3: I heard a large screech – the sound of tires stopping, heard people –

Girl 1: asking, "Is he alright," "What happened?"

Girl 2: I pushed my way through the crowd to see David bleeding. His eyes were open, and I thought –

Girl 3: ... he was sleeping. I stood, not moving, and watched from the sidewalk as they worked on my friend.

Girl 1: When I get home, my mom grabs me, happy to see me. Dazed, I wonder what his gift was.

Girl 2: I wonder how mom knew. She must have super powers.

Girl 3: That night I woke from a dream, my small hands cupped around his gift.

Girl 1: A small red heart – beating.

End of Scene

JENNIFER M. CUNNINGHAM

SAY IT RIGHT: USING DRAMA TO ILLUMINATE LANGUAGE DIFFERENCES

RATIONALE

In order to help pre-service and current teachers understand the difficulties that some students who are standard English learners (SELs) (Redd & Webb, 2005) have when translating from their home languages (for this particular workshop, African American Language) to standard academic English (SAE), a colleague and I created a workshop that includes an activity specifically addressing this issue. After introducing workshop participants to several common grammatical and phonetic features of African American Language (AAL) (Green, 2002; Palacas, 2001; Smitherman, 2006), we ask them to divide into groups and translate a portion of the graphic novel *The Way of the Rat* (Dixon & Johnson, 2004) from SAE to AAL. The following two tables[1] explicate specific grammatical and phonetic AAL features that we discuss in our workshop prior to the translation activity.

Participant translations, first of all, are literal translations, because we're expecting participants who don't speak or write in AAL to change the exact words phonetically and sentences grammatically. Authentic translations would not change word-for-word but more conceptually, including cultural nuances, vocabulary and slang. This activity further helps participants realize the grammaticality of AAL – there is a right and wrong way to speak and write in AAL, just as in SAE.

ACTIVITY

1. Once participants complete the portion of the workshop that introduces them to specific grammatical and phonetic features of AAL, they divide into groups of two or three and translate a portion of *The Way of the Rat* from SAE to AAL.
2. The portion of the novel is about 7 pages, and each group translates one page. We give groups about 15 to 20 minutes to translate their page, during our two-hour workshop.

---

[1] Tables 1 and 2 are adapted from Cunningham, J. M. (2010, forthcoming) jus showin sum luv 2 yo page: The digital representation of African American Language (Doctoral dissertation). Kent State University, Kent, OH.

J.K. Dowdy and S. Kaplan, Teaching Drama in the Classroom, 149–152.

TABLE I

Grammatical features found in African American language.

Grammar Feature	Definition	Example
Zero copula	In AAL the verb *be* and its conjugates – am, is, are, etc. – (represented as Ø), which would connect a subject and predicate in SAE, is absent.	What _Ø_ up? She _Ø_ still a punk.
Habitual *be*	The inclusion of *be* indicates regularity; the absence thereof indicates an isolated event.	I **be** bored. I **be** up at odd hours.
Agreement	In AAL there is no distinction between singular and plural verbs, and, therefore, no subject-verb agreement.	**You was** his only friend. **Is you** mad?
Negative concord	As with other languages, multiple negators are acceptable and used for emphasis.	I **can't** send you **no** message.
No possessive *s*	In AAL context rather than *'s* indicates ownership.	**Who ass** you fixen to go crazy on?

TABLE II

Phonetic features found in African American language.

Phonetic Category	Definition	Example
Consonant cluster configuration	Two final consonant sounds/letters in SAE are one final consonant sound/letter in AAL, if the final consonant sounds at the end of a word are both voiced or both voiceless (e.g., *st*, *nd*, *ng*).	**Jus showin** you some love. Hit up the **guessbook**.
Replacement *th*	The English *th* sound is replaced depending on voicing (voiced *th* or θ is generally replaced with *d* or *v* and voiceless *th* or ð with *t* or *f*).	Voiced: **Dey** about to go out. Voiceless: I'm so upset **wit** you.
Liquid vocalization of final *r* sound	Words ending in *r*, *er*, *or* or *ur* are replaced with a vowel sound.	I still ain't **yo** top friend. You is my **brotha** from another **motha**.
Monothong	Two vowel sounds pronounced in SAE may be pronounced as one vowel sound in AAL.	**Naw**, I didn't get around to doin it.

3. After translating, each group takes turns reading or performing their AAL translation, taking on the roles of the various characters.

Translation Example:

The Way of the Rat (SAE original)	The Way of the Rat (AAL translation)
Po Po: Wishing Dolls, Lost Treasure Caves, Monstrous Guardians. Why must PO PO's lot be entwined with a moron's?	Po Po : Wishin Dolls, Loss Treasure Caves, Monstrous Guardians. Why mus PO PO lot be entwine wit a moron?
Boon: Po Po? He seems frightened.	Boon: Po Po? He seem frighten.
Yan: Well don't scare him away again, Boon.	Yan: Well don scare him away again, Boon.
Jao: He's small, but there's meat on him.	Jao: He small, but dere meat on him.
Boon: It's not me scaring him.	Boon: Iss not me scarin him.
Po Po: Eep.	Po Po: Eep.
Boon: Something out … there …	Boon: Somethin out … dere …
Wing Tei Sun: The unwary will always find bad fortune more often than good.	Wing Tei Sun: Da unwary be finein bad fortune more often dan good.
Boon: What is this?	Boon: What dis?
Po Po: I did not think to ask its name!	Po Po: I ain't think to aks iss name!
Yan: We run, Jao!	Yan: We run, Jao!
Jao: There is nowhere to run, Yan!	Jao: Der nowhere to run, Yan!
Yan: Then we pray that Boon is a filling meal!	Yan: Den we pray dat Boon a fillin meal!

REFERENCES

Dixon, C. & Johnson, J. (2004). *The way of the rat.* Walls of Zhumar #21, CrossGen Comics.
Green, L. (2002). *African American English: A linguistic introduction.* Cambridge: Cambridge University Press.

Palacas, A. L. (2001). Liberating American ebonics from Euro-English. *College English*, *63*(1), 326–352.

Redd, T. M. & Webb, K. S. (2005). *A teacher's introduction to African American English: What a writing teacher should know*. Urbana, IL: NCTE.

Smitherman, G. (2006). *Word from the mother: Language and African Americans*. New York: Routledge.

HISTORY/SOCIAL STUDIES

JOHN YURKSCHATT JR.

GOVERNMENT STORY BOARD

RATIONALE

This activity provides students an opportunity to become educated about the three branches of the United States government. Over the course of the workshop students unite, partake in dialogue and collaborate to create a story board representing one of the branches of government.

Depending on the resources available to the students, access to three computers is useful. If computers are not available the instructor must provide students with multiple sources to research information for their assigned branch. Students are placed into one of three groups; the instructor assigns each group to research the Executive, Judicial, or Legislative branch.

Students then spend the next two or three days researching significant information about the branch of government which they were assigned. Once this research is concluded, students will come together with their ideas and create a large 4' × 4' story board, which includes a symbol of the branch as well as information critical to describing that branch in detail. The students have the liberty to include any information they deem important to inform the class about the branch of government which they were assigned. The teacher surveys the room on multiple occasions to make sure students are making progress and heading in the right direction. A story board is usually a sequence of events of a story/movie.

Upon completion of the story board, each group presents its story board and pertinent facts to classmates in a five- to seven-minute presentation. When all groups have presented, students free write for approximately five minutes on each branch that was presented. Students should include, in their free writing, all of the information they remember from the presentation. This allows the instructor to assess the knowledge gained by all students during this workshop.

Presentations are not given using conventional methods. Students have the option to convey their message to the class and teacher using the method(s) they choose, including any or all of the following:

- Create a skit
- Perform a song
- Recite a poem
- Use tableau
- Tell a story
- Perform a dance

J.K. Dowdy and S. Kaplan, Teaching Drama in the Classroom, 155–156.

Many students view government as boring or too far removed from their everyday lives. This provides students an opportunity to learn more about the government than they may through lecture or discussion.

WHAT TO DO

1. Instructor provides necessary resources for students (internet access or articles, books, etc.).
2. Students are selectively placed into three groups.
3. Each group is assigned a branch of the government.
4. Students begin research using various resources (instructor oversees dialogue and interactions).
5. Groups create story boards using provided poster material with markers, crayons, etc.
6. Groups will be given two to three full class days depending on progress to create their story board and to rehearse.
7. Groups reveal final product to all students during five- to seven-minute informative presentations.
8. Students take part in free writing exercise (five minutes for each branch of government).
9. Instructor assesses writings and creates lessons to include any critical information not mentioned.

RYAN MELIN

STEPPING INTO HISTORICAL PERSPECTIVES

RATIONALE

I am a secondary education major at Kent State University and was enrolled in Dr. Joanna K. Dowdy's Reading and Writing in Adolescence class. Her energetic, caring and passionate personality created an environment of acceptance that stressed the importance of adolescent literacy. The workshops she presented allowed the class to be creative and artistic, and she has greatly helped my instructional development by preparing me to use a variety of literature mediums in the classroom to promote reading and writing. The more she challenged my mind to visualize text as more than simply words on paper, the more my teaching tool belt expanded, and I began to construct interdisciplinary lessons for my future learners that addressed adolescent literacy.

I have always been interested in learning about history from multiple perspectives in order to see the event from more than one point of view. Most secondary school history textbooks used in the United States are written from a Western perspective, which I feel limits learners in truly understanding how history affects everyone in ways beyond what our vantage point permits. I believe that learners will understand the complexities of history better when they learn about it from multiple perspectives. I try to transmit my knowledge of history through the lens of not just the conquerors, but also through the lens of those conquered and all others impacted by an event. I first read the poem "A Worker Read History" by Bertolt Brecht while in Dr. Dowdy's class, and it is a good example of how I want my future learners to think about history.

This workshop was created in order for individuals to learn about a historical event from multiple perspectives. I created four scenarios that describe the same event from the view of four different characters. The class was to separate into four groups and study one of the scenarios, each starting with the words "You are" in order for the learners to know whose perspectives they were learning from. They were to use adjectives to describe how the scenario made them feel. Each group shared their feelings about their scenario with the class as a way to see the event from multiple perspectives and how the perception of any event is influenced by the viewpoint of those involved.

J.K. Dowdy and S. Kaplan, Teaching Drama in the Classroom, 157–159.

RYAN MELIN

WHAT TO DO

1. Read *A Worker Read History* by Bertolt Brecht to the class.
2. Interpret the message(s) conveyed in the poem. What point is the Bertolt Brecht making in the poem? Discuss how it conveys a multiple perspective insight to the nature of history and historical events.
3. Discuss historical events that the participants think have a seldom-told side to them.
4. Decide on a single event.
5. Brainstorm possible perspectives from which the event can be told.
6. Form into groups, one group per scenario, and three or four people per scenario.
7. Assign each group a character's perspective.
8. Each group write a descriptive scenario from their assigned character's perspective beginning with the "You are" and include the perspective of before, during, and after the event.
9. Share the scenarios with everyone.
10. Use the messages, emotions, and ideas expressed from the poem and scenarios to discuss how historical events can be similar and/or different depending on whose perspective the event is told from and why it is important to consider multiple perspectives.

SAMPLE SCENARIOS

Scenario One

You are a worker for the Mansa. Your entire life you have worked in the gold trade, and a few years ago you began to take gold to distant trading centers for the Mansa. You love trading and working with the gold, but the trips across the unforgiving desert are difficult, long and dangerous. You are rewarded for your excellent work by being selected as a member of Mansa Musa's caravan to Mecca. You are traveling with the most gold in your life, and you dream about all the possible goods to be traded. When you arrive at the end of the 3,000 mile journey and enter Mecca, Musa begins to throw handfuls and handfuls of gold into the streets and hands out even more to the high officials. You leave Mecca with no new goods.

Scenario Two

You are Mansa Musa. You prepare for your pilgrimage to Mecca by assembling a huge caravan with Mali's finest creations and hundreds of pounds of gold. You are greeted warmly upon entering Mecca and meet many people and see many new things. You give away your gold to random people in the streets and more along with other gifts to officials, as evidence of your wealth and goodness. You leave Mecca after visiting all you wanted and return home. Your pilgrimage has

158

been a positive personal experience. Also, it has been a positive experience for your empire. You have shown the wealth, prestige and power of your empire to the world. Now, everyone is talking about the amazing Mali Empire and how it is the best place in the world.

Scenario Three

You are a merchant in the city of Mecca. There is rumor of a faraway king coming to visit your city. You hope he is friendly and you'll be able to make money from the visitor. You witness Mansa Musa generously giving gold to everyone. You receive some of the gold and are very happy. A year later the value of gold has been deflated dramatically. The trading market is in chaos, and your business is not producing as well as it used to. To purchase any goods costs twice the amount of gold compared to before Mansa Musa's pilgrimage. You are having trouble providing the essentials for you and your family and might have to move.

Scenario Four

You are a merchant in the city of Timbuktu. You and your family are happy living in Timbuktu. The trading market is not only prosperous for you and other citizens but also the city. Your standard of living is supreme with a large home, surplus of food and goods, and excellent schools. The extreme wealth shows in the city's architecture, magnificent public and religious buildings, and top-of-the-line education. Your business continues to thrive while Musa is away on his pilgrimage. Upon Mansa Musa's return from Mecca you hear that he has made many friends and that your city is now on the map in the rest of the world. You talk to some citizens who went on the pilgrimage and they tell you everyone loved them so much that many newcomers are going to come live in Timbuktu.

JANET HILL & ANTHONY L. MANNA

EXPLORING HISTORY'S HUMAN DIMENSION WITH PROCESS DRAMA: RUBY BRIDGES AND THE STRUGGLE FOR SCHOOL DESEGREGATION

On November 14, 1960 a brave six-year-old girl named Ruby Bridges entered William Frantz Elementary School as the first black child to ever attend school there. Prior to this historic event, there had been a lot of talk on both sides of the racial divide. Parents – both black and white – were worried and afraid for their children. Would their children be safe? Did parents want to sacrifice their children for the sake of equality? Why was it necessary to change the status of the way things had always been? What would the neighbors think? These questions and many others haunted the minds of parents in New Orleans, Louisiana in the fall of 1960. Their concerns figure into the process drama we present in this chapter, in which we ask students to take on the roles of these New Orleans parents. The goals of this drama are to help students understand the conflicting points of view, the sacrifices people made and the historical impact of desegregation.

Process drama is a teaching and learning strategy through which students of all ages examine pivotal human issues and reflect on classroom content, while also developing social and communication skills (Wilhelm and Edmiston, 1998). As its name suggests, process drama encourages students to become engaged in a process of entering the lives of imagined characters and analyzing events from their perspectives. Participants assume roles and respond to events through the focused lens of a role they have co-created with their teacher's guidance. Process drama emerged in the 1960s from earlier educational drama methods in which students prepared brief skits and teacher-directed scenes that typically culminated in some type of performance by small groups of students, thereby revealing their understanding of content and concepts. While teachers might use some short-term activities such as role play to enhance student exploration of a drama's themes, in process drama these activities serve as tools and not as ends in themselves.

In a process drama, students co-create and move through a series of interconnected teacher-developed episodes that function as the structure for the events to be interpreted and the roles students adopt (O'Neill & Lambert, 1982; Miller & Saxton, 2004). Within these episodes, the teacher invites students to improvise the dialogue, action and interaction that will help them gain a greater understanding of the social condition, human event or subject matter they are investigating. To provide students a genuine platform for learning, teachers often need to carry out research to ensure the accuracy of the information that figures into a particular

J.K. Dowdy and S. Kaplan, Teaching Drama in the Classroom, 161–170.

episode. At times, the teacher puts a drama structure on hold and has the students themselves engage in research to strengthen their roles, integrate essential details and deepen the drama's tensions. Research is particularly crucial when a drama sets students on a course that leads to discoveries about a historical event, such as the desegregation drama in this chapter (Wilhelm & Edmiston, 1998).

While the structure of a drama provides a sturdy guide for the development of the episodes, process drama teachers also capitalize on the improvisation that evolves as a result of students' ideas and actions while they are in role. In fact, teachers encourage students to contribute to and shape the drama based on the discoveries they are making about the topic being explored.

Teachers facilitate the action of the drama either from outside the drama or within it. Working outside the drama, they serve as catalysts that are removed from an episode but instrumental to its development. In this capacity a teacher might be a narrator who establishes the setting for the drama or provides information about the historical incident that drives the drama's action, as, for example, the narrator does in the introduction to our Ruby Bridges drama.

When process drama teachers facilitate from within a drama, they join the improvisation and collaborate with their students by taking on a relevant role. The status, tone and attitude the teacher assumes when in role serve as clues for the students in figuring out their own status and keeping the action or conflict alive. In the drama structure provided in this chapter, the role the teacher uses to involve students is that of an informed leader conducting meetings about desegregation in his or her church. When teachers enter the drama process in role, they are participating not as actors but rather as guides or storytellers intent on helping their students engage with the drama topics – such as the intricacies of historical incidents, the lives of story characters, the problems in scientific controversies, school policies, political debates or space travel. The intent here is not to develop student (or teacher) acting skills or create a polished performance. Rather, in process drama, participating in role should allow students and teachers to use their imaginations and, in the heat of the moment, to face and learn from the ideas discovered through their active involvement in each episode.

Several process drama elements we describe here are at work in the drama structure we created about Ruby Bridges. This drama reveals the social and political tensions that brought responses to school desegregation to a feverish pitch when the United States federal government ordered New Orleans schools to desegregate in 1960. Supported by the NAACP and federal law, Ruby Bridges endured hostile crowds of white adults who daily taunted her as she made her way to the white school. While Ruby Bridges does not play an active role in our drama, the complex moral and political themes evoked by her situation become the challenges participants in the drama confront as they move into the roles of both black and white New Orleans residents who are deeply concerned about the repercussions of desegregation for themselves and their children. Here issues of right and wrong, moral responsibility, and individual, family and racial identity come into play.

THE RUBY BRIDGES DRAMA

The Drama Structure	Commentary
	Terminology: In the 1960s, when this drama takes place, the common term for African Americans was the word Negro. Therefore Negro is used in this drama. Prior to presenting the drama, teachers may want to review changes in racial markers and their implications with their students (http://bit.ly/jpHGL).
(Slide of "Segregation Hurts Children")	*Visual Images*: In this drama, we incorporate electronic slides projected on a wall or a large screen. A visual aide helps to spark interest, set a tone and provide a context for the drama. The visual provokes curiosity and stimulates the imagination, providing a context for the question, "What is going on here?"
Teacher as Narrator: On November 14, 1960 New Orleans Federal Judge Skelly Wright ordered the public schools to desegregate. For 6 years following the *Brown vs. the Board of Education* decision, the Orleans Parish School Board had delayed desegregation in their schools through a series of lawsuits and appeals. After Judge Wright's order, the School Board reluctantly gave in, resulting in Wright and his wife being shunned by their friends and neighbors. Judge Wright's effigy was hung outside a New Orleans high school, and the Wrights were reviled by the powerful people in society.	*Teacher as Narrator*: The teacher is establishing a context for the drama. In drama, a pivotal moment in history such as this is called a pretext. A pretext is a door that leads to exploration, a crucial moment that has a past and a future. Think of the pretext as a starting point, as the lead to the tension (O'Neill, 1995). In this drama the pretext is that moment when parents are working through the issues that define the problems surrounding the integration of schools and making decisions about their own children's future. The narration here sets the stage for what is to come by giving historical background of desegregation in New Orleans. By focusing on the Wrights' problems, this narration gives a human dimension to the conflict and, in turn, puts a face to what otherwise might be cold historical fact.

Episode One *Place*: Church Meeting – Zion AME Church, New Orleans, LA. *Participants*: Black members of the church.	*Episodes*: Dramas are divided into episodes. Each episode develops the pretext and is placed strategically in a planned series. However, the sequence might change depending on the unexpected course the improvisation may take as the drama unfolds (Miller & Saxton, 2004).
Teacher in Role: Friends, we have just received news that a child in our congregation, Ruby Bridges, has been selected as one of four Negro children who will integrate the Orleans Parish school system. As you know, the order for desegregation was issued six years ago, but the wealthy white folks in this state have figured out ways to keep it from happening. Now Judge Wright has ordered the School Board to be sure that every school in Louisiana is integrated by November 14. I know many of you feel that it is wrong for us to place this burden of integration on this little six-year-old girl. Some of you feel we should not go where we aren't wanted. Some of you, who have experienced racist violence, fear that the children will be hurt by the angry white folks. What are some of you thinking about sending this little girl to integrate the schools?	*Teacher in Role*: The teacher, in role as the leader of the congregation, gives clues to the students as to how they will want their own roles to take shape. At this point, the teacher in role invites the students into the drama by asking them to express their opinions based on the life experience of the characters whose roles they have chosen to assume. For instance, some of the students may wish to take the perspective that the community shouldn't go where they are not wanted, as suggested by the teacher in role. In a sense, the teacher is developing a story line that the students will join by moving into their own roles. Students will need to pay attention to the voice, tone and content of the teacher's role in order to develop their own identities and relationships within the episode. The question of sending a six-year-old girl to integrate the school brings to the foreground the moral obligation of the future of desegregation. In a process drama teachers layer opportunities for involvement in order to deepen the student commitment to the issues at hand.

(Show slide of Johnson Lockett Elementary School)
Teacher in Role: You are all familiar with Johnson Lockett Elementary School. Most of you attended this school. You probably see your own children or grandchildren in this photo. What are your memories of going to school here?

Slide: The use of this visual gives the participants a point of reference to help develop the improvisation. By showing the slide of the black school, the teacher invites the participants to dig into the past to generate memories of attending that school. This serves to bind the group together and develop their understanding of the characters. By showing a historic photograph, the teacher instills the drama with a sense of reality, which helps to expand students' belief and involvement in the drama event.

(Show slide of the William Frantz Elementary School)
Teacher in Role: This is the school where little Ruby will attend first grade. I don't think any of us has ever seen the inside of this building, except Harold here, who worked as the janitor for 25 years, and Celina, who used to pick up little Jimmy, the child of the woman she worked for. What do you think school will be like for Ruby and those who follow? Is this what we want for our children? Now Ruby's parents have agreed to let her go to this school, because she will get a better education. What these people are doing is going to affect your children, your grandchildren and every black child who goes to school from now on. In spite of what you may feel about the situation, this brave family needs our support. What can we do to support them?

At this point, the participants are in role as black people looking into the world of the white school. By facing the white world head on, the participants are examining the complex consequences that may occur from these actions.

Following the discussion, the teacher in role thanks the group for attending the meeting.

Teacher as Narrator:

Ruby: My parents argued about what to do. My father, Abon, didn't want any part of school integration. He was a gentle man and feared that angry segregationists might hurt his family. He didn't think that things would ever change. He didn't think I would ever be treated as an equal. Lucille, my mother, was convinced that no harm would come to us. She thought that the opportunity for me to get the best education possible was worth the risk, and she finally convinced my father.

Lucille says: Ruby was special. I wanted her to have a good education so she could get a good job when she grew up. ... There were things I didn't understand. I didn't know Ruby would be the only black child in the school; I didn't know how bad things would get.

These actual quotations from Ruby and her mother (Bridges, 1999) bring into the drama voices that increase the believability of the drama world by providing tangible evidence of its reality (Wilhelm & Edmiston, 1998).

Episode Two
Place: Mount Zion Methodist Church, New Orleans, LA.
Participants: White members of this congregation.

Teacher in Role: Friends, thank you for coming to this meeting. We are all here because we don't agree with our neighbors who plan to withdraw their children from William Franz when the Negro girl begins school next week. Now you all know that, as your pastor, I have been very outspoken about integration because I believe that every child has a right to a good education. I know you're here because you want to do what's best for your children and the community. Most of our neighbors

Episode: Each episode drives the drama forward. The teacher decides on the number of episodes needed to play out the pretext. While this demonstration drama is very short, most dramas usually incorporate many episodes.

Sometimes they can go on for weeks, depending upon the purpose and the path the teacher and students may want the drama to take. Here the participants are invited to switch their perspective from that of a black person to that of a sympathetic white person. The foundation of this drama is built on this switching of perspective and what insights can be gained from playing out different points of view. This brings to light the many sacrifices that white families made to threaten to remove their children from school if a Negro child attends. What have they been saying about this situation? I've talked to some of you, and I know you want your child to stay at William Frantz, because you believe that integration is the right thing to do. Some of you have said that you just won't be bullied by those folks who are applying pressure to empty the school of white children. What are your reasons for wanting to keep your child in the school?

remain true to their beliefs. Here the teacher's tone is a strong voice for social justice. This gives the students a clue as to the position that these group members have taken.

By keeping our children in school we are putting them in grave danger. We know that those radical segregationists will stop at nothing to get the attention that will fuel their hatred. I'm wondering, though, what we are going to do. Do we have a choice? Can we take the risk of our children being hurt? Of us losing our jobs? Of our property being damaged?

Questioning is a significant strategy for giving information, maintaining role and providing direction within the drama. The questions are carefully chosen to help students shape their thinking and respond as group members in role. This fosters interaction among the students and the teacher. Questions provide momentum to keep the drama moving, because they inspire critical thinking and involvement (Miller & Saxton, 2004).

Final Episode:

Teacher as Narrator: While Ruby was preparing to attend William Frantz, several white families were determined to send their children as well. One of them was the working-class Gabrielle family who believed that it was right to integrate. Every day, they walked their daughter Yolanda to her first-grade class facing the threats, taunts and even rotten eggs hurled by the white protesters.

In this drama, it is important to point out that everyone who made a commitment also made a sacrifice.

Teacher as Drama Leader: Let's think about this family and what they went through for the sake of their convictions. What words might come to their minds when they encountered these hostile people?

Teacher writes the descriptive words on the board.

You can imagine all the photographs that were taken by news photographers during this time. Let's create a photograph of this scene of Yolanda's parents walking their daughter to school and the people they must have met along the way. The teacher asks volunteers to create the scene as a still-life called a "tableau." As the volunteers come to the space where the tableau is going to be shown, the teacher can work with the students regarding characters and their placement in order to best show the conflict.

Teacher as Drama Leader: Recording descriptive words helps students prepare for what is to come next, in this case an activity known as "tableau."

A *tableau* is a brief rehearsed nonverbal performance activity in which small groups of students represent the thoughts and feelings of a person or group of people in the form of a still-life. Tableau has multiple uses in the classroom, including extending the understanding of classroom content, abstract ideas or the specific features of an event. In a large class, the teacher may wish to form several groups to create individual tableaux that will then be presented to the class. While a group is performing its tableau, other students serve as an audience that responds to each tableau (Manley & O'Neill, 1997).

(Slide of Ruby entering school)

Step into the Slide: Students volunteer to step into the slide and talk to Ruby as she enters William Frantz School for the first time. They may give her words of encouragement, support and admiration. *Teacher:* This is the end of our drama.

Stepping into the slide: This is an activity that allows the students to become a part of history. As the slide is projected on a wall in a "larger-than-life" format, students place themselves in the projection path so that the silhouettes of their bodies and/or heads become a part of the slide (Smith, 2006). This creates an intimate point of view through the physical stance that the students take and also what they say (History Alive! http://www.historyalive.com).

Reflection: Students are asked to respond to the drama experience while it is still fresh. The teacher asks students, "What will you take with you from this drama? What do you still wonder about this event in history?"

Reflection is an essential part of the learning process. It helps the students strengthen their understanding of what has just taken place and make connections with contemporary issues. As the discussion continues, the teacher might want to project a summary slide of the episodes to help refresh the students' memories. The teacher should encourage the students to make connections with contemporary issues. Discussion may take on concepts such as

- Bullying
- The clash of differing principles and values
- Standing up for what one believes is right
- The value of looking at an issue from another point of view
- Present day examples of prejudice, social injustice and racism.

APPENDIX: VISUAL IMAGES USED IN THE DRAMA

- Slide 1: School Segregation Protest – Black adults and children are carrying signs that read "We Protest School Segregation" and "Don't Treat our Children Like Prisoners." Internet source: http://commons.wikimedia.org/wiki/File:School_segregation_protest.jpg.
- Slide 2: Southern Black School shows a large white rural school building. The tin roof is damaged and missing in some places. The paint is peeling and the siding has come off in places. Black children are posing in the play yard by the school. Internet source: http://members.fortunecity.com/babyboomer/fifties/fifties017.jpg.
- Slide 3: William Frantz Elementary School appears as a large brick fortress. The school name is carved into the lintel. White parents are taking their children up the stairs into the school. Source: Bridges, R. (1999). *Through my eyes*. New York: Scholastic, p. 13.
- Slide 4: A detective escorts Yolanda Gabrielle and her mother Daisy past a heckling crowd. Source: Bridges, R. (1999). *Through my eyes*. New York: Scholastic, p. 29.
- Slide 5: Ruby entering William Frantz Elementary, escorted by three U.S. Marshals. Ruby, whose back is to the viewer, looks very small in contrast to the Marshals and the monumental arch around the door of the school. Source: Bridges, R. (1999). *Through my eyes*. New York: Scholastic, p. 42.

REFERENCES

Bridges, R. (1999). *Through my eyes*. New York: Scholastic.
Manley, A. & O'Neill, C. (eds.) (1997). *Dreamseekers: Creative approaches to the African American heritage*. Portsmouth, NH: Heinemann.
Miller, C. & Saxton, J. (2004). *Into the story: Language in action through drama*. Portsmouth, NH: Heinemann.
O'Neill, C. (1995). *Drama worlds: A framework for process drama*. Portsmouth, NH: Heinemann.
O'Neill, C. & Lambert, A. (1982). *Drama structures*. Portsmouth, NH: Heinemann.
Robinson, P. (1995). A house divided: A study guide on the history of civil rights in Louisiana. Retrieved November 1, 2009, from The Southern Institute for Education and Research Website: http://www.southerninstitute.info/civil_rights_education/a_house_divided_index.html.
Smith, B. (2006). Write here, write now. Conference workshop presentation. Northeast Ohio Writing Project. Kent State University. July. Kent, OH.
Wilhelm, J. & Edmiston, B. (1998). *Imagining to learn: Inquiry, ethics, and integration through drama*. Portsmouth, NH: Heinemann.

AMANDA JANOSKO

ECONOMICS (MACROECONOMICS)

TOPIC: CONTROLLING THE U.S. ECONOMY

Objective: Students will be able to identify figures and organizations within the U.S. economy. From this lesson students will be able to list the key organizations and individuals who help create the United States' monetary and fiscal policies, describe the relationships between them, understand what each is responsible for and present their findings to the class. This subject matter is important because economic decisions made by both the Federal Reserve and figures in Washington affect the individual lives of students, their families and the larger community.

PROCEDURE

1. Students are split into small groups of three or four. The teacher can assign these groups, have students count off into groups, or choose their own groups, depending on the class.
2. Each group researches an individual or organization assigned by the teacher, perhaps based on difficulty or personal interest of the student. Figures and organizations for this research should include people heavily involved in the economy during any given period of time: Ben Bernanke, Timothy Geithner, FOMC, Barack Obama, the Senate, the House of Representatives, etc.
3. Students are given time to research their topics at the school library and are encouraged to use multiple media types, including the internet, newspapers, magazines and books. Written text as well as pictures and audio resources may all be used.
4. Students should use reputable sources that are well cited. They should look for information that describes who each person/organization is, what duties they have and how they affect the larger economy.
5. Each group is then responsible for relaying who that person/organization is and what their role is through a dramatic performance. Students can present this information in an interview fashion, like the abbreviated example below, or they can create a skit that depicts their given person/organization.

Evaluation: Students are evaluated on their dramatization. Some questions a teacher may want to reflect on when evaluating this project include the following: Did students accurately relay the information they learned during research about their individual/organization? Did they explain their person's/organization's role

J.K. Dowdy and S. Kaplan, Teaching Drama in the Classroom, 171–172.

in the economy? Did students create a well planned thought-out presentation? Did all group members participate? Ideally, students show understanding of who/what their person/organization is and what larger significance they have.

Materials: Paper, writing utensils, textbooks, access to school library and props.

An abbreviated example skit:

Person 1: I have a job.
Person 2: What is your job?
Person 1: I work as an economist.
Person 2: Well, where do you work?
Person 1: I work at the Federal Reserve.
Person 2: What do you do there?
Person 1: I help create monetary policy for the nation.
Person 2: What's that?
Person 1: It's policy that targets the federal funds rate to help stabilize the economy.
Person 2: What is your name again?
Person 1: I'm Ben Bernanke.

KELSEY POORMAN

ADDRESSING VISUAL CULTURE THROUGH SCRIPT WRITING

INTRODUCTION

Visual culture and the media dominate a large part of current society's interactions in public and private settings. It is essential that students be taught visual literacy, so that they develop the ability to think critically about the media and how it affects their lives. Media activists are artists that produce artwork, usually in the form of 'subvertisements', using media advertising techniques that challenge the cultural influence of commercialism. Media activists are driven by the idea that they can use their artwork in a similar fashion as propaganda and voice their opinions on issues.

Subject: Script writing for a drama

Topic: Media Activism

Objective: The student will write a scripted dialogue about an interview that he or she is conducting with a media activist artist.

PROCEDURE

1. Discuss what media activism is through a Power Point presentation and class discussion. Students will also look at several examples of works done by artists regarding media content. Check for comprehension during and after presentation.
2. Students look at sample scripts and the assignment is explained to them.
3. Students brainstorm in groups, questions they would want to ask a media activist and create possible responses.
4. Students write out script and check for errors (dialogue).
5. Students assign roles and determine lines. They also choose setting and any props needed.
6. Students rehearse script in groups.
7. Students perform script in dramatic form in front of class.
8. Class gives feedback and discusses significance of activity through a series of guided questions related to what students have learned on the topic.

J.K. Dowdy and S. Kaplan, Teaching Drama in the Classroom, 173–174.

Evaluation: Read students script and observe drama (participation is key).

Materials: Paper, artworks, pencils, space for acting, space for rehearsing, props, electronic devices needed for Power Point and examples of scripts.

KAREN ANDRUS TOLLAFIELD

LIVING HISTORY: USING DRAMA IN THE SOCIAL STUDIES CLASSROOM

RATIONALE

Teachers hear the term "differentiated instruction" more and more these days, and administrators expect it to be an everyday occurrence. Using drama in conjunction with other strategies is an effective way to utilize various learning styles to help students process content. One such strategy is "Living History."

Being able to "live" history allows students to immerse themselves in a particular place and time and take on the mindset of someone who lived then. In this way students are engaged and interacting with the material rather than passively watching and listening.

After the dramatic representation, students' discussions, writings and understanding of that historical place and time are much deeper than when they simply read about it or watched a film.

WHAT TO DO

1. The teacher projects an image from the historical period being studied onto a large white bed sheet or piece of paper using either an overhead projector or document camera. The sheet should be hung from about six feet high down to the floor, and the image should be life-sized.
2. Students "step into the picture" by creating a tableau in the poses of the projected images right in front of the sheet in order to take on the voice of the person/people in the setting. The dialogue can be done in many ways, but the most common is to let the students stay in the pose for a few seconds and try to "become" the person in the photograph and to feel what he or she would be feeling.
3. Students are then asked to begin a dialogue with one another as these people and to discuss what is going on both inside their heads and around them. In this way students can demonstrate knowledge of content, creativity and even empathy.
4. After students have had the opportunity to voice their subjects, the instructor may follow up with discussion, readings and writing assignments.

This strategy can also be used as a preview for new teaching material when the students are asked to do this before they have learned about the historical events

J.K. Dowdy and S. Kaplan, Teaching Drama in the Classroom, 175–177.

of the period. They see if they can figure out what is going on and what these people might be thinking about and saying to one another. It might be interesting to see how the dialogue changes if this strategy is used both before and after the students are familiar with the material. In essence, this strategy works well either as a preview or review of a lesson and may even be used as an assessment of comprehension.

It is important to note that the first time this strategy is used in the classroom, the students may be a bit shy or may not know what to say; therefore, it is key for the teacher to model it for the students. Once they have an idea of how this works, they will love "living" history.

SAMPLE

This lesson was used in a fourth-grade classroom in a cross-curricular Science/Social Studies unit. We had been studying the effects of weather on land and learning about the 1930s.

Figure 1. Photo courtesy of the Library of Congress

THE DUST BOWL

After reading about the Dust Bowl era of the 1930s, I projected the picture shown above onto a sheet to make it life-sized. In groups of four, the students took turns stepping into the picture and taking on the poses of the projected images to become a still tableau, giving them time to become the character.

Once comfortable in their new skin, they used their new knowledge from the reading material and our classroom discussions to actually voice what these people might be thinking.

After all the students had an opportunity to "live" history, they wrote letters as displaced persons living through this time and moving to California, wrote letters to friends "back home" in Oklahoma. The experience of speaking as the people in the pictures gave an authenticity to their letters that did not emerge when I had done this lesson in previous years without using this strategy.

MARIANNE THOMAS-JACKSON

BRIDGING THE GAP BETWEEN WRITING & ORAL HISTORY THROUGH RESEARCH AND DRAMA

RATIONALE

To encourage diversity and acceptance of difference through writing and sharing personal cultures I created this project to include in College Writing II. As a black woman who embraces culture, I feel a responsibility to encourage an acceptance of the diverse nature of culture and to incorporate that acceptance into the framework of writing, especially as it relates to peer-to-peer evaluations. Understanding that the average college student comes into College Writing with several "fears" intact, I create a learning-friendly atmosphere by pairing students right away. These pairs are instructed to share the usual types of information with one another: names, hobbies, majors and goals, etc. After the first week of school the students are instructed to share information regarding their family cultures and make weekly entries in their journals about their partner's culture.

Throughout the semester I rotate students so that they have the opportunity to work with as many of their peers as possible. Their most important project is to develop through research and interviews with family members a clear picture of the types of negative stereotyping their particular culture has been subjected to. After they have developed both research and journal entry skills, the students are required to work with a group of four to five students designing a dramatic skit that depicts a scene of cultural stereotyping, the effects negative stereotyping has on a family or on a person's ability to gain equal access to education, jobs and the "American Dream." The students use their knowledge of diversity awareness to create another scene in which they attempt to repair through dialogue some of the damage created by negative stereotyping.

This activity hones research and writing skills of college students, creates an atmosphere of community, and also prepares the college student to become familiar with and accepting of a diverse worldview. In addition, creating a space where students can freely learn about and embrace their own personal cultures encourages diversity at its most critical level: a student's self-awareness and self-esteem.

STEPS

1. The teacher has students share their particular cultures with the entire class.

J.K. Dowdy and S. Kaplan, Teaching Drama in the Classroom, 179–181.

2. The teacher selects five essays that discuss negative stereotyping and oral history. Two good examples are *In the Kitchen* by Henry Louis Gates, Jr. and *No Name Woman* by Maxine Hong Kingston.

3. The class discusses some similarities of characters from all cultures represented in the essays.

4. The teacher has students choose two (personal family) cultures and brainstorm ideas for creating scenes of negative cultural stereotyping and dialogue that might result in positive perceptions of their different cultures.

5. Students are paired to create and write scenes.
   Goals and Objectives: To begin dialogue regarding the effects of negative stereotyping on particular groups and possible avenues through the writing process to change one's mindset regarding "cultural difference" as it relates to societal disdain towards particular groups. In addition, I believe that one cannot fully embrace diversity through cultural exchange if one is unaware of his or her own unique culture.

   — Scenes should be between two and three pages.
   — Specific place and time.
   — Contain appropriate dialogue.

6. Students act out their scenes.

7. Students write a three-page reflection on their experience.

Note: If there is not a positive resolution at the end of a scene, each student should be prepared to brainstorm reasons for this and share with the class.

SAMPLE

My culture consists of African American, Native American and Southern white. Since I have the least knowledge of my Native American heritage, I chose to begin my research with interviews of family members with any oral history to share. Armed with some memories from my maternal grandmother, I researched historical data and Ancestry.com in order to create a bridge between oral history and actual documented written histories.

I learned that my great-great maternal grandmother, Sarah, was part Cherokee and was married to my great-great grandfather, Will Daniels, whose father was white and mother was a slave. It seems that Sarah was mistreated by whites and stereotyped as a "savage" because of her reddish skin and long straight black hair. Will was also mistreated and was almost shot by an older white man when he entered the man's store through the front door instead of waiting on the back stoop as was required of blacks. The scene I wrote depicted an incident much like the one when Will was almost shot, called derogatory names and dragged out of the store by his feet as his wife Sarah was being held on the ground by other white men.

My scene dealt with the anger that a black man felt when ostracized, belittled and was unable to protect his wife from the whims of white men. I created an old, black Christian woman who mentored the married couple and was able to teach them to pray for strength and courage to survive such desperate, dangerous times. This old woman introduced them to a compassionate white couple who eventually led them to the North where they learned that not all whites were evil and not all blacks were angels. The message in this scene was that "difference" does not create license to misuse or disparage a human being, but rather every person is entitled to embrace who they are without fear of violence or discrimination by the dominant culture.

CREATIVE PLAY

YUKO KURAHASHI

HUNTER-HUNTED: AN ENGAGEMENT EXERCISE

RATIONALE: FINDING CONNECTIONS WITH OTHERS WHILE USING ALL OF ONE'S SENSES TO BE AWARE OF THE ENVIRONMENT

This exercise has been used to build rapport among the participants (students) as well as to raise their awareness of their surroundings. Too often people forget to be aware of their environment and other people. Yet, paying attention to one's environment is an essential tool in human communications, including acting. Many theatre educators find it important to develop an actor's senses not only as a fundamental element of acting, but also as a tool to learn how to truly engage with others and build trust for future collaborations.

This exercise was handed down through multiple instructors and students. I learned it from a graduate student in acting, whose instructor (also my colleague) taught it in his acting class. He was initially introduced to the exercise in his undergraduate program from a professor who might have learned it during his graduate program. This chain of instruction itself is an important example of human communications, demonstrating the awareness, among the educators, of the importance of developing interactions and communications in the classroom and beyond.

This exercise also challenges our habit of over-depending upon visual information as a learning tool. In this exercise, one is asked to complete the mission without using his/her eyes. The participants must use their other senses. It also introduces the basic format of becoming a presenter/performer. The selected individuals are asked to "perform" the required task while the rest observe them. By physically experiencing this basic "presentation" format, the students are prepared for future public presentations and performance, while the "observers" learn how to be attentive and supportive of the presenter.

WHAT TO DO

1. The class is divided into two groups who sit on opposite sides of the room, forming a row on each side.
2. From each group, the instructor chooses the hunter from one side and the hunted from the other. In the selection process, everyone needs to close his/her eyes.
3. The selected hunter and hunted are asked to keep their eyes closed. The instructor throws a "weapon" (a rolled newspaper, for example), in the middle of the exercise area and announces "the hunt begins."

J.K. Dowdy and S. Kaplan, Teaching Drama in the Classroom, 185–186.

4. The hunter, with eyes closed, searches for and grabs the weapon with which he/she pursues the hunted.
5. The hunted (with eyes closed) travels from the original side to the other and sits on the hunter's chair. Then the game concludes (the winner, in this case, is the hunted).
6. Repeat this process with different pairs.

KELLY BRETZ

GUESS WHO I AM? DRAMA AND WRITING

RATIONALE

This activity was created to give students an opportunity to improve their drama and writing skills. It also allows students to use their creativity in writing in order for them to become a particular character or inanimate object involved in a certain event. In order to better comprehend any text being read, a student needs to think as if he or she were actually experiencing the events in a story. Sometimes these events don't necessarily involve a human being but rather animals or even inanimate objects. This activity enables students to create unique narratives which involve sensory details and imagination, in order for them to better understand a character's point of view and the actual event in a story. This activity is also good for the students who do not feel as comfortable as others doing drama activities in the classroom. These students are still able to do the drama activity, but they can keep it to themselves if they choose to.

MATERIALS

- envelopes that contain scenarios written on slips of paper
- scenario sheets
- sheets of paper
- pencils

PROCEDURE

1. Students are told that even though people experience the same types of events, their points of views can differ. For example, the pigs in the story "The Three Little Pigs" have a different idea about what happened in the story than the wolf would, even though they were all experiencing the same events.
2. Students are given the scenario sheet and read it quietly to themselves.
3. Students then have a discussion on how one person or object may have a different point of view from the object or person across from it. An example is a parent having a completely different idea from the child of how the living room window became broken.

J.K. Dowdy and S. Kaplan, Teaching Drama in the Classroom, 187–189.

4. Students then get into pairs, and each is handed an envelope, in which there are two different slips of paper. One has one person or object on the list, and the other has the other person or object relating to the same scenario. For example, one person will have a police officer and one will have a thief.

5. The students then need to get out a piece of paper and write a narrative about their character's point of view about a situation, without giving their character away. They have to use sensory details (sight, hearing, smell, taste and touch) while they are writing. For example, if a person has a fish, then he or she should write about how it swims all day, all it sees is cloudy water and should not to swim toward a shiny hook with a delicious worm on it. This is also a good way for students to become non-human objects and to make them come to life.

6. After students write for a few minutes, the teacher calls on a pair of students. Each student reads his or her narrative. After listening to both narratives, the class has to guess who or what they are, based on the scenario sheet.

7. The activity concludes with a reflection on how hard or easy it was to become each person or object.

SCENARIO CHOICES

(Copy, cut and place in envelopes)

baby	diaper
fish	baited worm
firefighter	person in a burning building
parent	child
person	cell phone
student	teacher
deer	hunter
golf ball	golf club
dog	dog catcher

person	mirror
person	Thanksgiving turkey
snowman	sun
police officer	thief
feet	shoes
performer	audience

MARIANNE SCHULTZ

DRAMATIC WRITING

This lesson is an excellent way to excite students about writing. Students often state that they don't like writing – it's too difficult to brainstorm a story, they don't know how to spell words, they can't think of anything else, or it's just boring. This is a more interactive way to make writing come alive through the use of props and then acting out written stories with students' own bodies. Students are writing if-then books modeled after the *If You Give a Mouse a Cookie* series.

I like to use this activity in my first-grade classroom because it gets even my shyest writers excited! They have the opportunity to create ridiculous stories and are excited about them. When the stories are completed, they don't mind the grueling task of editing them, because they are looking forward to acting the story out for their classmates. They are challenged to think about how to use their own body to act it out. This is why, even though I use this with my first-graders, it is not until the very end of the year, and I recommend it for more experienced writers, too, such as second- and third-graders.

The stories the students create are always interesting since they pick the animal and have very few parameters other than making sure the objects or activities relate to each other. I'm always impressed by the creativity of the students, and it seems to be helpful especially to those children who dislike writing. They have this opportunity to write down silly things and usually create a successful writing piece. In addition, those students who are shyer get the experience of being in front of the classroom but as a different "character," which helps them gain confidence. One must remember that this is an ongoing lesson that may require a week's worth of time before students feel confident enough to share their stories with the class.

WHAT TO DO

1. The teacher reads several if-then stories aloud to the students. ("If You Give a Mouse a Cookie," "If You Give a Pig a Pancake," "If You Give a Moose a Muffin," etc.)

2. The teacher discusses what happens after each item is given, pointing out the "ifs" and "thens" in the story. He or she asks why, if a mouse has a cookie, it would want a glass of milk, making sure to point out that these items are

J.K. Dowdy and S. Kaplan, Teaching Drama in the Classroom, 191–192.

related, because when you eat cookies, your mouth gets dry and you want something to drink.

3. When students have a good understanding of the if-then story, they can brainstorm some if-then statements. (For example, if I run a red light, then I will be pulled over by the police. If I eat too much candy, then I will be sick.)

4. Next the teacher points out that in the if-then stories, the ending frequently echoes the beginning. So if you go to the fridge for a glass of milk, you will probably want a cookie to go with it, etc.

5. Each student decides on an animal he or she would like to be.

6. Each student is given a prop (see ideas below). Students brainstorm an if-then story based on their animal and the prop. For example, if I choose to be an elephant and my teacher gives me a marker, my story would follow: If you give an elephant a marker, then he will want some paper to color on. But when he gets the paper to color on, it will be too small and he will accidentally color the floor. So he'll want you to get him a mop, and then he can clean his mess. After he cleans his mess, then he'll be hungry and ask you for a peanut butter sandwich ... This story may be shared with the class to help some students brainstorm a first sentence.

7. Students write their story over the course of several days.

8. When students have completed their stories, they act them out using no props while the teacher reads them aloud to the class.

MATERIALS

Anything for props (marker, ball, apple, shoe, etc.), writing paper, and if-then books.

ADDITIONAL ACTIVITIES/ MODIFICATIONS

- If students struggle with writing their stories, the teacher can put them in groups to write their stories.
- Students act out the original stories.
- Students brainstorm alternative items the characters in the original stories might want.
- All students act as a mouse, crawling on the ground and imagining that everything is much larger than they are. They discuss their feelings and write a new if-then story from a mouse's perspective.

JOANNE KILGOUR DOWDY

POETRY IS MOTION

The Poetry Is Motion workshop is a series of exercises that lead students to develop multiple representations of poetry and visual art. This article examines the
use of multiple forms of communication in the language arts classroom through
interpretation of images, poetry writing and dramatic expressions that follow
from the creations. Using ekphrasis as its foundation, the exercises included
are designed to facilitate visual literacy skills, enhance new literacies and use
the students' life experiences to create meaningful communication. Students are
encouraged to bring their reading of the world to the space where the word is
the foundation of their skillful use of multiple sign systems. The implications
for enhanced interpersonal communication skills through the expression of their
insights about human personalities support the efforts to facilitate students in
developing and sustaining meaningful interpersonal relationships.

THE POETRY IS MOTION WORKSHOP SESSIONS

In workshops for pre-service and veteran teachers, we facilitated the use of multiple forms of expression using the expressive arts by introducing participants
to poetry performance and creation of dramatic interpretations of original word
creations.

Following are the steps that the teachers followed during the Poetry in Motion workshop. We facilitated the skills that helped students work with art as a
prompt for their writing and acting (Dowdy, 2009). First, the learners created
autobiographies for the characters they discovered in the pictures that we showed
them. Then, we had them interact with each other in character. Finally, they were
encouraged to create poems based on their analysis of the pictures and the characters represented. Adjustments were made to the sequence of steps as students
began to feel comfortable with each other and started experimenting with their
characters in improvised scenes.

PROCEDURE

1. Participants chose one of the images presented. Images can be chosen from a
   calendar, a collection of magazines that represent different cultures or posters
   for books that the students are reading or have seen on display in the library.

J.K. Dowdy and S. Kaplan, Teaching Drama in the Classroom, 193–196.

2. In groups the participants decide how best to represent the image in tableaux. The tableau is a frozen frame, like a picture, that represents a moment in time. This exercise is exactly like playing "statues" so that others can read the scene.
3. Groups look at each other's pictures to see each group's interpretation of the image.
4. Each person creates a character sketch for the person whom they represent. Answering the questions who, what, when, where and why about the character in the picture that they choose helps each student talk about the imaginary character's background.
5. Each person, in character, tells a short story about who he or she is and what he or she is doing in the tableau when asked to speak to the whole group in character.
6. The group rehearses an improvised conversation among the characters that represents what is happening in the scene which the tableau represents.
7. Each group shares its scene with the whole class.

CYCLE OF THE CHARACTER'S STORY

In order to create a character's history, the class is invited to go through an activity that includes a series of creative writing exercises. These steps for students include the following directions:

1. Choose a character from the image that you are using as a prompt. If we use the young girl on Greenfield's book cover, we have a character to work with.
2. Decide on a crisis event or wounding, learning or discovery that your character experiences in the course of his or her life. For example, if the young girl on the cover has had a parent die when she is 10 years old, it would be considered a wounding event. Students try to fill in as many details as possible about the critical event that the character has endured. Use the who, what, when, why, where questions to help fill in the facts about the young girl.
3. Finally, create a scenario in your mind's eye about the way in which the critical incident is now applied to the character's life, i.e., how does the young girl described above use the learning or discovery to resolve new crises? The students write as much as they can about this learning and its application to the character's life.

For example, when we read the poem "For Strong Women" by Marge Piercy (1980), I picture a woman who has had to face many obstacles in life. I choose a picture from a magazine or another visual source that makes me think of the kind of woman who represents determination in the face of adversity. The crisis this woman faced in her childhood was the death of her mother and the consequent separation from her siblings. The brother and sister had to live with a grandmother and uncle until they finished high school. This wounding event, the death of her mother and then the destruction of the nuclear family, leads the woman in my poetic imagination to be a caring, motherly, protective adult. She takes on challenges on behalf of those she considers powerless and unprepared to survive under trying circumstances.

WRITING THE IMAGE

1. Look at a selected image. For example, if you look at the cover of Greenfield's (1978) book of poems, you can focus on the profile of the child's face.
2. Write down a noun, two adjectives, three action verbs, a four-word sentence, and finally another noun, that you think about as you look at this image. Example: Girl, happy, kind, running, skipping, laughing, she moves like wind, sunshine.
3. Write a complete sentence using the nouns, adjectives and verb that you have chosen to associate with this image. Example: A happy girl who skips, runs, and laughs like she is full of sunshine.
4. When you are finished, share your sentence with a partner.
5. Work with two other people to pool your sentences together. Each of you should write down all the sentences for the three of you who are now a team. As a team, decide which of the nouns, verbs and adjectives will become the chosen words for your next creation. As soon as that choice is made, you can go ahead and collaborate on a new sentence. The new sentence may look like this because of the additions from two buddies: A young black girl laughing at the sun, skipping with her friends. She is Honey, sweet and good and light brown, too.
6. Decide on a name for your creation. Look at the story that you have pieced together. How can you label the experience that the reader will have once she takes meaning of your sentence? Example: Childhood.

At the end of this sequence of steps I alert students to the fact that they have cycled through three versions of the same ideas that the original image prompted them to think about (Romano, 1995). First, they created a poem with the selection of verbs, nouns and adjectives. Then they made sentences, another symbol, that led to paragraphs representing the thoughts about the image and what it meant to them. Finally, the groups came up with a title for their written creation (Thomson, 2003). This label conjures images in the mind of the reader just as the first picture created certain associations with past and present emotions and experiences interacting within the authors (Rosenblatt, 2005).

REFERENCES

Dowdy, J. K. (2009). From poems to video script. *Excelsior: Leadership in Teaching and Learning*, *3*(2), 56-71.

Greenfield, E. (1978). *Honey, I love and other love poems*. New York: HarperCollins.

Piercy, M. (1980). *The moon is always female*. New York: Knopf.

Romano, T. (1995). *Writing with passion: Life stories, multiple genres*. Portsmouth, NH: Boynton/Cook.

Rosenblatt, L. (2005). Literature-S.O.S.! *Voices from the Middle*, *12*(3), 34-38.
Thomson, L. M. (2003). Teaching and rehearsing collaboration. *Theatre Topics*, *13*(1), 117-128.

ABOUT THE AUTHORS

Anthony L. Manna is an Emeritus Professor at Kent State University in the departments of English and Teaching, Learning, and Curriculum and Instruction. His research interests include children's literacy development, process drama, and children's and young adults' interactions with literature.

CHARACTER DEVELOPMENT

Yuko Kurahashi is an associate professor of theatre, Graduate Coordinator, and AOT (Art of the Theatre) supervisor in the School of Theatre and Dance at Kent State University. Dr. Kurahashi is the author of *Asian American Culture on Stage: The History of the East West Players* (Garland, 1999) and *Multicultural Theatre* (Kendall/Hunt, 2004 & 2006).

Joanne Kilgour Dowdy is a Professor of Adolescent/Adult Literacy at Kent State University in the department of Teaching, Learning, and Curriculum and Instruction. Her major research interests include women and literacy, drama in education, and video technology in qualitative research instruction. Her other credits can be found at jkdowdy.com.

Sarah Kaplan is the Drama Director at Theodore Roosevelt High School in Kent, OH. She also teaches English, Acting, and Play Production. Sarah earned her Bachelor's degree from Ashland University in 2004 and her Master's in Education from Kent State University in 2009.

William Kist is an associate professor at Kent State University, has been researching classroom uses of new media for over a decade. His profiles of teachers who are broadening our conception of literacy were included in his two books, *New Literacies in Action* and *The Socially Networked Classroom*, focusing on the uses of Web 2.0 in the classroom. Dr. Kist remains active as a new media artist himself–nominated for a regional Emmy for music composition, he is developing his own screenplay, *Field Trip*. Dr. Kist blogs at www.williamkist.com, and he may be followed on Twitter at: http://twitter.com/williamkist.

J.K. Dowdy and S. Kaplan, Teaching Drama in the Classroom, 197–201.
© 2011. *Sense Publishers. All rights reserved.*

Sandra Perlman is an award winning writer whose plays have been produced at The Cleveland Play House and New Jersey Repertory and published in several anthologies. A graduate of American University, Perlman has taught English in grades 9–12 and playwriting at Case Western Reserve and Cleveland State Universities.

MUSIC

Sandra Golden is Assistant Professor of Education at Defiance College. She teaches undergraduate and graduate level literacy courses. Dr. Golden's research interests are literacy development, culturally relevant pedagogy, and multicultural education.

Jennifer Hauver James is Assistant Professor in the Department of Elementary and Social Studies Education at the University of Georgia. Her research interests rest at the intersection of teacher biography and pedagogical decision making, and include efforts to understand the power of dialogue, reflective inquiry, community engagement and the arts for fostering democratic education.

Susan Van Deventer Iverson is an Assistant Professor of Higher Education Administration & Student Personnel at Kent State University where she is also an affiliated faculty member with the Women's Studies Program. Her scholarly interests include gender, equity, and diversity in higher education, change-oriented experiential pedagogies, and the use of feminist poststructural research.

Diana Awad Scrocco is a doctoral student in Rhetoric and Composition at Kent State University in the Department of English. Her research interests include workplace literacy, multimodality in education, and digital composing.

Terry Boyarsky is a concert pianist, singer, Ethnomusicologist and teacher of Dalcroze Eurhythmics. She is trained by the Kennedy Center in arts integration and is a Teaching Artist with Young Audiences of Northeast Ohio and the Ohio Arts Council. She presents Movement & Music workshops internationally. Currently she performs and tours as "Russian Duo" with a balalaika virtuoso from Siberia.

ADAPTING LITERATURE

Karen Greene Seipert has taught English Literature and Composition at the college and high school level. She has a BA and MA in English Literature, as well as IB certification in Language A1. Karen is completing her doctorate in Educational Technology in early 2011.

Carie Greene has taught all grades from first through eighth and all subjects during her 25 years as a classroom teacher and proficiency specialist. She has taught introductory education classes at Wayne College/Akron University and is a certified Hatha Yoga teacher who has instructed yoga classes for five years at various locations, including Kent State University, the Cuyahoga Valley Environmental Education Center, and the Bergamo Conference Center.

Jaclyn Consilio teaches English at Theodore Roosevelt High School in Kent, Ohio in the Career Technical Education Department. She earned her Bachelor's Degree in Integrated Language Arts (7–12) from The University of Akron and her Master's Degree in Curriculum and Instruction from Kent State University.

Heather Oris earned her Master's Degree in Curriculum and Instruction from Kent State University. Currently, she is teaching high school English at Theodore Roosevelt High School in Kent, Ohio. She may be reached at ke_horis@kentschools.net.

Mary Toepfer is an adjunct professor at Hiram College in the English and Education departments and at Kent State University in the department of Teaching, Learning, and Curriculum and Instruction. Her major research interests include improvisational drama, literacy strategies across the content areas, and process writing.

Teri Poulos teaches English at John Glenn High School in New Concord, OH. She earned her Bachelor's Degree in English Education from Michigan State University and her Master's Degree in Curriculum and Instruction from Kent State University.

Brandy Mcfee is a graduate student at Kent State University, studying Curriculum and Instruction. She is also a language arts teacher for Rootstown Local Schools in Rootstown, Ohio. She has taught for six years, in grade 7 for 5 years and one year teaching 9th and 10th grade.

Jessica Cervenak is a graduate of Kent State University with a Masters Degree in Curriculum and Instruction. This is her ninth year teaching English, Speech, Journalism and Humanities at Waterloo High School in Atwater, Ohio. In addition to teaching, she is also the high school newspaper adviser.

STORYTELLING

Jacqueline Peck currently teaches literacy education classes at The University of Akron. She is an experienced storyteller with teaching experience in middle childhood public school classrooms. She has numerous publications in literacy research and teaching.

Rhonda S. Filipan is a doctoral student in Higher Education Administration at Kent State University. Her dissertation will be a narrative inquiry into the lived experiences of women who teach as part-time and non-tenure-track faculty in the academy. She frequently uses journal writing, script writing, and fictional characters to untangle personal and professional issues in her own life.

GOOD IDEAS

Steven L. Turner is an Assistant Professor of Middle Childhood Education in the Department of Teaching, Learning and Curriculum Studies at Kent State University. His research is focused on the learning sciences (how people learn) and investigating how high-stakes tests influences instruction and learning. Please direct all correspondence to sturner6@kent.edu.

Carol L. Robinson is Associate Professor of English at Kent State University. Her research focus is upon visual and aural communication semiotics. She teaches freshman composition, film and literature, medieval British Literature, and American Deaf literature. She also serves as a liaison between Deaf and hearing individuals on the Trumbull campus.

Nancy M. Resh is a full-time Instructor of American Sign Language at Kent State University. Her research includes ASL literature and, in particular, her growing collection of Deaf community stories. Other work includes development and promotion of leadership within the Northeast Ohio Deaf community, as well as serving as a liaison between the Deaf and hearing.

Daniel-Raymond Nadon is an Associate Professor in Theatre at Kent State University, where he specializes in Community Based Theatre, Multi-cultural Theatre and LGBT Theatre. He received his Ph.D. from the University of Colorado and was one of the first recipients of the Fulbright Grant to work in Quebec, Canada.

Mary E. Weems is an African American poet, playwright, imagination-intellect theorist and foundations of education scholar. Books in include Public Education and the Imagination Intellect: I Speak from the Wound in My Mouth (Peter Lang, 2003) and a book of poems titled An Unmistakable Shade of Red and the Obama Chronicles (Bottom Dog Press, 2008). Weems is currently an Assistant Professor in the Department of Education and Allied Studies at John Carroll University in University Hts., Ohio.

Jennifer M. Cunningham is an English composition instructor at Stark State College and is finishing her doctoral dissertation "jus showin sum luv 2 yo page: The Digital Representation of African American Language." Her chapter was inspired by workshops she presents to students and teachers about the validity of African American Language.

200

John Yurkschatt, Jr. is a graduate student at Ohio University where he is pursuing his Master's degree in Cultural Studies. His major research interests include project-based learning and multicultural education.

Ryan Melin is an undergraduate student, majoring in integrated social studies with a concentration in history at Kent State University in the department of Teaching, Learning, and Curriculum Instruction. His major interests include Colonial America and African history, poetry and visual art in education, and nutrition literacy.

Janet Hill is from Delaware State University where she teaches courses in literature and literacy. She has been helping people develop understanding of texts and life through drama for many years.

Amanda Janosko is a senior integrated social studies major at Kent State University. She is currently completing her student teaching and will graduate in the spring of 2011.

Kelsey Poorman attends Kent State University. She is majoring in art education and hopes to teach high school art.

Karen Andrus Tollafield has taught elementary and middle school students for 30 years, specializing in Language Arts for the last 20. She is a National Writing Project Teacher Consultant, and a PhD student at Kent State University in the area of Curriculum & Instruction: Literacy.

Marianne Jackson, MFA, is a non-traditional Black student, with five children and nine grandchildren. She is currently a PhD student teaching College Writing at Kent State University. She enjoys writing Poetry, Fiction and Plays.

CREATIVE PLAY

Kelly Bretz is currently a teacher at Southington Middle School in Southington, Ohio. She has taught kindergarten, first grade, fourth and fifth grade reading and is currently a fifth and sixth grade intervention specialist. She received her bachelor's degree from Youngstown State University and her Master's degree in Reading Specialization from Kent State University.

Marianne Schultz is a graduate student at Kent State University, studying Curriculum and Instruction for a degree in Reading Specialization. She has been teaching four years at Hickory Ridge Elementary in Brunswick, Ohio where she is a first grade teacher.

9 789460 915352